freedom fighters

The essential handbook for living
in the victory of the cross of Jesus Christ.

sherri ohler

Published by 39 Baker Drive, Geneva, IL 2017

Copyright © Sherri Ohler 2017

ISBN: 978-0-9911122-6-5 (E-Pub)
ISBN: 978-0-9911122-5-8 (Trade Paperback)
ISBN: 978-0-9911122-7-2 (Kindle)

Cover design © 2022 Sherri Ohler
Editing by Stacy Lepley
Chapter opening picture design © 2017 Sherri Ohler

The author asserts the moral right to be identified as the author of this book.
*Some names and identifying details have been changed to protect the privacy of individuals.
Scripture quotations marked (NLT) are taken from the Holy Bible, New Living Translation, copyright © 1996, 2004, 2007 by Tyndale House Foundation. Used by permission of Tyndale House Publishers, Inc., Carol Stream, Illinois 60188. All rights reserved.

Scripture quotations marked (ESV) are taken from the Holy Bible, English Standard Version. ESV® Permanent Text Edition® (2016). Copyright © 2001 by Crossway Bibles, a publishing ministry of Good News Publishers. All rights reserved.
Scripture quotations marked (NASB) are taken from the New American Standard Bible Copyright © 1960, 1962, 1963, 1968, 1971, 1972, 1973, 1975, 1977, 1995 by The Lockman Foundation, La Habra, Calif. All rights reserved.
Scripture quotations marked (BSB) are taken from The Holy Bible, Berean Study Bible, BSB

Copyright ©2016 by Bible Hub
Used by Permission. All Rights Reserved Worldwide.

Scripture quotations marked (NIV) are taken from The Holy Bible, New International Version®, NIV® Copyright © 1973, 1978, 1984, 2011 by Biblica, Inc.® Used by permission. All rights reserved worldwide.

Scripture quotations marked (WEB) are taken from The World English Bible is a 1997 revision of the American Standard Version of the Holy Bible, first published in 1901. It is in the Public Domain.

Scripture quotations marked (KJV) are taken from the Holy Bible, King James Version. It is Public Domain.

All rights reserved. No part of this publication may be reproduced, stored in a retrieval system, or transmitted in any form or by any means, electronic, mechanical, photocopying, recording or otherwise, without prior permission of the publisher or author.

Contents

Acknowledgments v
Dedication vii
Introduction 1
Our First Weapon: Salvation 3
    We Have All Chosen Death 4
    The Shedding of Blood 4
    Enter Jesus, Savior of All Who Will Have Him 5
Weapon Two: Repentance 6
    Repentance Part One 7
    Retire and Return 7
    Rest 7
    Repentance Part Two 8
    Nothing in Common with Satan 9
    Our Sins Are Many 9
    If We Confess Our Sins 10
    Power in the Tongue 10
    Detestable Things 11
    Sins of Commission 11
    Sins of Omission 12
    Generational Sins 13
    Prayers of Repentance 14
Weapon Three: The Three Baptisms 17
    Baptism with Water 18
    The Old Testament Pictures of Water Baptism 18
    Jesus's Baptism 20
    Faith Filled Prayer for Water Baptism 21
    Baptism with the Holy Spirit 21
    But I Thought I Received The Holy Spirit at Salvation? 24
    Baptism with Fire 25
    Kings Protecting Their Crowns 29
    Persecution 29
    Promotion & Praises 30

- Your Personal Persecution 30
- The False Fire 31
- Weapon Four: Forgiveness 33
  - What Forgiveness is NOT 34
  - Supernatural Forgiveness 35
  - What Does Forgiveness Have to Do with Freedom? 37
  - How to Forgive 38
- Weapon Five: Inner Healing 40
  - My Wake Up Call to the Need for Inner Healing 41
  - Offending the Holy Spirit 42
  - Identity 43
  - Connecting to the Healer 44
  - The Deep Truth of Psalm 46 45
  - What is This River? 47
  - Loved Children Shouldn't Beg 48
  - Each Other 48
  - Time to Heal 51
  - Step 1-Worship 51
  - Step 2-Naming the Symptoms 53
  - Step 3-Uncovering the Rotten Roots 53
  - Seeing 54
  - Feeling 54
  - Memories/Flashbacks 55
  - Healed Memory Example 55
  - Conclusion 56
- Weapon Six: Deliverance 58
  - So, What Exactly is Deliverance? 59
  - Can a Christian Have Demons? 59
  - Logic 60
  - Possessed? Oppressed? Something Else? 61
  - Two Ways to Be Delivered 62
  - Knowing the Demon's Name 62
  - What Deliverance Ministry is Truly About 64
  - The Devil's Method of Deliverance 64
  - Is Deliverance Ministry Dangerous? 65
- A New Calling: Spiritual Warfare 68
  - The Blood of the Lamb 69
  - Communion 69
  - The Word of Their Testimony 72

Acknowledgments

Father, Jesus, Holy Spirit, there are not enough words to write, praises to sing or gifts to give to express my gratitude for all You are and how You have pursued me. I am nothing without Your love, grace and sacrifice. Thank you for letting me write for and be a part of your glorious kingdom. I'm forever in awe of YOU.

Randy, my best friend and biggest prayer warrior- thank you for believing in and supporting me always and in every way. Without you, this book and so many other things, would not be possible!

October, Ivy & Cheney-Thanks for bringing me so much joy and for listening to my Jesus stories even when you think I'm a little crazy. Someday you'll thank me for all the times I rebuked something for you! Haha!

Stacy, thank you for all your prayers and for forcibly removing all my commas to make sure this book was its absolute best!

Dedication

For everyone who has ever struggled to find joy and peace in this thing we call life. May you find your answer in relationship with the One who knew you before you were you.

And for Ella, my little freedom fighter.

Yes, Jesus LOVES you...

Introduction

"And from the days of John the Baptist until now the kingdom of heaven suffereth violence, and the violent take it by force."

(Matthew 11:12 KJV)

     This tends to be one of the most misunderstood verses in all of the New Testament. People associate violence with negativity so rather than wrestle with Jesus to find out what in the world He was trying to say, they glance over it and move on because it seems to contradict the faith and theology they have been embracing thus far. But after just a slight pressing in to the original Greek that it was written in, a world of understanding opens for every believer to embrace the key to victory in each area of life. The depth and revelation in this one small verse is echoed throughout both the Old and New Testaments and is directly in line with God's character. It is the summation of a true biblical worldview in just one sentence. And here it is, simplified.....

     "...and the violent take it by force." The word 'violent' can also be translated 'STRONG', the phrase 'take by force' is actually just one word–'*harpazō*'. It means 'to snatch away', to 'pluck', 'pull' or 'catch away' and it implies 'forcefully and quickly'. It is the same word used to describe the rapture of the saints when we are 'caught up' with Jesus in the sky instantaneously. *(1 Thessalonians 4:17)*

     So what does all of this mean? The kingdom of heaven is suffering under violent attacks of satan, and those who are strong in Jesus will take it back from him forcefully.

     We are in a WAR. From the time of John the Baptist until now the kingdom of darkness has declared an all out war on the Kingdom of Light, God's people. Since he can't touch God, Satan is actively, aggressively making the Kingdom suffer by violence, and we are told by Jesus to TAKE IT BACK, by force.

This book is filled with the revelations and tested methods I have learned from the Lord directly and through others that will teach you how to take back by force what the enemy has stolen in your personal life, and in the bigger picture of the Heavenly Kingdom as a whole. It is not an exegesis of all of scripture, and it does not claim to be an exhaustive teaching on any one aspect of our life in Christ. Rather, it is an overview of each step we walk living in the full victory of the cross, along with some powerful methods of daily spiritual warfare found in scripture. From salvation & baptism, to healing & deliverance, to walking in the power of the Holy Spirit to set others on the same freedom path, we are about to embark on a life changing journey that will turn the tables on the enemy of our souls and keep us on the victory path in every arena. We are declaring ourselves Freedom Fighters in God's Kingdom and we will not stop until we see Him on the day of His return. THIS is what life with Jesus is all about. Grab your sword of the Spirit and let's roll....

OUR FIRST WEAPON:

SALVATION

"...if you confess with your mouth, "Jesus is Lord," and believe in your heart that God raised Him from the dead, you will be saved. For with your heart you believe and are justified, and with your mouth you confess and are saved. It is just as the Scripture says: "Everyone who believes in Him will not be put to shame."

(Romans 10:9-11 ESV)

The temptation as I write this chapter is to prove that Jesus really is Savior of all who will have Him, but this is not that book. There are many such books on the subject of the validity and infallibility of the bible as well as the history of Jesus's time on earth along with the eye witness accounts (more than five hundred!) of His resurrection. So I will resist the temptation to delve into apologetics and just get to the point; If one wants to live free, one must believe in and verbally profess the death and resurrection of Jesus Christ as the only means for justification and salvation. Period.

We Have All Chosen Death

In a nutshell, the Creator of all made us in His image with free will and a choice of life or death. Every human on the planet starting with Eve and her husband, Adam, has chosen death. What brings death? Anything less than the holiness, righteousness and justice that we were created to walk in. The Holiness, Righteousness and Justice that is our Creator.

The beautiful thing is that He did not leave us on our own to try to figure out the path to life and death, He spelled it all out from the very beginning. Adam and Eve had just one rule, *"...but of the tree of the knowledge of good and evil you shall not eat, for in the day that you eat of it you shall surely die." (Genesis 2:17)* Up to that point the creation of humanity knew no evil, we were holy, righteous, just and able to walk with our Father who created us for relationship with Him. But at the first bite of the fruit of that one tree, our spirits died with the knowledge of evil. We chose poorly, and lest you tell yourself that it is all Eve's fault, the truth is that each of us ever since have chosen to know evil again and again.

The Shedding of Blood

The act of choosing to know evil through the eating of that fruit opened a floodgate of depravity on the earth and the ways to defy our Creator went from just one to countless. With that evil came death, and with death came the shedding of blood. Death was never God's will for us, He told us not to go there, remember? But our choice of spiritual death begot the need for physical death to atone for what we had done. Our perfect Creator is JUST. Without consequences to our choice of death, He could not be called Righteous and Just. In the same way that a judge who lets a murderer go would be seen by us as unjust, if the Creator let acts of defiance slide He would not be perfect, yet He is. Without consequences, there is no justice, without justice, there is no love. *"The LORD loves righteousness and justice; the earth is full of his unfailing love." (Psalm*

33:5 NIV) To make this example real to us we need just to think of the last time somebody hurt us or a loved one and got off scott free, the love of justice that was put in us by our holy Maker urges us to want recompense, some kind of re-payment to make things right. In God's holiness the only repayment possible for choosing spiritual death, was physical death and the shedding of sinless blood.

The Old Testament law of the shedding of animal blood was a temporary means of atonement for God's chosen people, the Jews, it was a mere foreshadowing of His plan to redeem all mankind from the clutches of Satan, back from death, back to life and rightful relationship with Himself.

> *"We...know that a man is not justified by works of the Law, but by faith in Jesus Christ."*
>
> *(Galatians 2:16)*

Enter Jesus, Savior of All Who Will Have Him

Fully God and fully man, Jesus came and died as the ultimate and final payment for every choice of evil that every man or woman has ever, and will ever make. This amends by Jesus for our rebellion against our holy Creator is what we call SALVATION. It is a confession from our mouth that Jesus chose to shed His blood in physical death in our place, that in love He came to die for us as a means to satisfy the need for perfect JUSTICE. It is the belief in our hearts that because He was raised from that death and went before us into Heaven to the right hand of the Father that we are forever JUSTIFIED and will not be put to shame. The last words of Jesus on the cross were, *"It is finished." (John 19:13)* Salvation is the first and most important of all the steps to walking in freedom, for without it none of the other steps can be.

Weapon Two:

Repentance

"For thus the Lord GOD, the Holy One of Israel, has said, "In repentance and rest you will be saved, In quietness and trust is your strength.""

(Isaiah 30:15) (NAS)

Repentance Part One

Repentance really is used as a freedom tool throughout our lifetime, but as you can see by the scripture above there is no salvation without this step which is why it is step number two. Steps one and two go hand in hand but since repentance without a Savior is moot, it by default needed to come after Salvation. This original step of repentance that leads to salvation along with the profession of Christ's death and resurrection is Part One.

Retire and Return

The Hebrew word for repentance in the scripture above is 'shûbâh', the incredible meaning behind this one little word that has the power to change eternity for individuals and nations alike is- retirement, and returning. If we mean what we say when we profess that *"Jesus is Lord"*, then we will be willing to retire from our life of evil and return to His ways of holiness and righteousness as defined in the scriptures. This step of leaving our old life behind as we profess Jesus is the mark of a true Christ follower. When He truly is our Lord, we want to please Him and walk where He is, in holiness. Jesus himself even said,

> *"And you will perish, too, unless you repent of your sins and turn to God."*
>
> *(Luke 13:3 NLT)*

Retire and return. There is no other way.

Rest

What we retire from is evil, and what we rest in, as stated in the same breath of Isaiah in the scripture above, is the belief that Christ's death on the cross has justified us completely. We repent/retire from our life of sin, and then we rest from all efforts to self-justify. (*"It is finished."*) This is where the 'belief in your heart' really matters. We REST both from self righteousness and self abasement, we rest from searching for man made answers and instead seek after deeper understanding of Jesus. We rest from fear of what comes 'after' and revel in the promise of heaven, we rest from the false humility of shame and with true humility, by grace take our position of honor in the Kingdom, we rest from seeking identity in earthly things and embrace our new identity as accepted and loved son or daughter of the One True King, and it is from this new identity that all freedom in this life is realized.

You will find that when you enter this rest everything in your soul sweetly and finally exhales. It is the assurance of salvation and purpose and it is what you have been searching for your whole life without knowing it. This is your first taste of the freedom of the cross.

Repentance Part Two

> *"Search me, O God, and know my heart: try me, and know my thoughts: And see if there be any wicked way in me, and lead me in the way everlasting."*
>
> *(Psalm 139:23-24 KJV)*

This is my shower prayer. It seems only fitting to get spiritually clean at the same time that we take care of washing our physical body, right? The word tells us that God's mercies toward us are new every morning (Lamentations 3:23). We should take Him at His word and seek Him every morning to make sure that we are cleaned on the inside and left pure and holy in Jesus. When we ask Him to reveal any wicked way in us, He will.

Our initial turning from sin in repentance allows us to enter into the Lord's salvation and it is a beautiful thing. But in order to be fully free and victorious over the enemy, we must now take repentance to the next level with verbal proclamations and confessions of the sins that we are turning from.

Nothing in Common with Satan

Our goal of freedom requires living each day having NOTHING in common with the enemy, just like Jesus lived.

"...for the ruler of this world comes, and in Me he has nothing." (John 14:30 BLB) Other translations read, *"...he has no claim on me."(ESV)*, <u>*"...he has no power over me." (NLT)*</u>, *"...he has no hold on me."(NIV)*

The message is simple, if we want to live in the freedom of Jesus Christ, we are to give the devil no place within us, so that he will have no claim or hold on us, and no power over us. Our acts of evil have given Satan and his demons legal rights to us, we must revoke their rights. This is accomplished through REPENTANCE.

Our Sins Are Many

Before we come to believe in and profess Jesus as Savior, most of us choose acts of evil everyday. You may have heard this referred to as 'sins of commission', in other words we are committing these acts by conscious choice. From lying big and small to hate and gossip, from fornication, adultery and sexual perversion such as homosexuality or masturbation to not honoring our mother and father or coveting our neighbor's wife (and life!), from seeking other gods to worshiping self by creating our own personal version of god-the sins we choose are many and unfortunately, more and more commonplace in the world we live in. Most of the aforementioned acts of evil are portrayed in entertainment as normal and embraced as part of everyday life. But even if we are not committing all of these ourselves, we praise and cheer them on or in the least condone them in the lives of others. Imagine that, cheering on acts of evil that will keep people bound in the very darkness that we ourselves wish to escape from. So heartbreaking, but we have all done it haven't we?

We come to the Lord having everything in common with Satan, and the Lord loves and accepts us with open arms anyway, but now that we are aware of our filthiness it's time to take a spiritual shower. This initial 'prayer shower', so to speak, will last awhile for most of us, a few hours is pretty likely. Just keep praying Psalm 139:23-24 and as things come into your mind confess them in a declaration of your retirement from each act and returning to the Lord in new life. Do this over and over until there are no more sins that surface in your mind as you pray.

I will give an example of an effective repentance prayer at the end of this chapter.

After the first time, these cleansing repentance showers should be pretty brief because we have already cleaned up from our pre-Jesus past and going forward, by the power of the Holy Spirit we no longer choose evil like we used to. *(1 John 5:18)*

If We Confess Our Sins

"If we confess our sins, he is faithful and just to forgive us our sins, and to cleanse us from all unrighteousness."

(1 John 1:9 KJV)

The key words here being 'if we confess'. The heretical belief that the whole world is saved by the cross regardless of if one acknowledges Jesus or not, regardless of if there is repentance or not- is debunked in this one small verse. We MUST confess our sins, and once we do, He gives, and we choose to receive His faithful forgiveness. Without the acceptance of His gift of forgiveness there is no true rest nor salvation. This goes back to that 'believe in your heart' matter. Jesus is enough. No matter what you've done, Jesus is enough, and after repentance you must accept the Father's gift of forgiveness to cover your sins. For some it may be helpful to ask Him to give you a picture of yourself or a word or phrase of how He sees you after you have been forgiven. Then when the enemy comes back to throw those old sins at you, you will have a supernatural picture or spoken word of the power of the cross to rebuke him with. Satan's attempts to shame you will then become a powerful weapon against him as you praise God for the blood of Jesus that took away your sins. The enemy will hate that and will eventually stop playing the shame card.

Power in the Tongue

"Death and life are in the power of the tongue..."

(Proverbs 18:21 ESV)

It is our tongue that brings life, therefor these confessions with repentance need to be out loud declarations. Something happens in the heavenlies when we speak. God created the entire universe and everything in it by speaking, and He has put a measure of that same power in our tongue.

According to James 5:16 it is wisdom to do this with another believer-

"Therefore, confess your sins to one another and pray for one another, that you may be healed."

(ESV)

But there are also many instances in the bible where repentance is a time of deep soul cries alone with God. Psalm 51 is a great example of this.

Detestable Things

"Do not bring a detestable thing into your house or you, like it, will be set apart for destruction. Regard it as vile and utterly detest it, for it is set apart for destruction."

(Deuteronomy 7:26 NIV)

This is an Old Testament scripture talking about an actual house and an actual object, and this still holds true today, but even more, we are the house of God, our bodies according to 1 Corinthians 6:19, are actually the temple where the Holy Spirit resides. More on that in a later chapter, for now I bring up this scripture to show that when we intentionally bring anything evil into our lives, we also welcome destruction. There are books that list every sin one could ever think of so that people can walk through each one in repentance, I believe those are a good starting point to see what God considers evil until we can fully grasp the entirety of scripture ourselves, but if we blindly just go down the list, A. We are not actually confessing in truth, and B. We may end up picking a fight with demons that we had never opened a door to before. Everything we do in regards to our walk with the Lord should be Holy Spirit led. If we pick up a book or list and declare war on the enemy by proclaiming everything it says, we are doing so in our own power, don't do that. It is wisdom to pray Psalm 139:23-24 in asking the Lord to lead us in exactly what we need to repent of, He will answer.

Sins of Commission

Sins of commission are sins committed by decision. Here is how it works, the enemy throws a temptation thought at us to lust, let's say, in that moment we have a choice to make to rebuke the temptation in Jesus's name and walk away in resistance, or to accept the offer to sin and follow the thought forward into fantasy and/or action. Think of it like this, evil knocks, that is the thought, merely a temptation but not a sin, we can either batten down the hatches, take that thought as our prisoner and hand it over to Jesus *(2 Corinthians 10:5)* and refuse to open the door so we stay pure and clean, or we can let him entice us into opening the door so he can come in and we can enjoy the sin. It is OUR choice. The word says in 1 Corinthians 10:13 that God provides a way of escape from every temptation. That is good news for those who take it, bad news for those who do not because it shows that we alone are culpable for our choice to commit evil and bring destruction. The real freedom of the cross of Jesus Christ means that we are living life free from fighting these constant battles of temptation. The word says that we are to submit ourselves to God (If you have picked up Weapon One and Weapon Two-then you have done this!) and resist the devil, then he will flee. Satan and all his demons will literally run for safety! From YOU! How amazing is that? *(James 4:7)* The original Greek word for resist is '*anthístēmi*', it means to 'set oneself against' or 'OPPOSE.' When you first come to Christ, or before you know how to reach freedom, you will have to set yourself against Satan's temptations to sin as you learn all these weapons of freedom fighting, but in a very short time as you keep reading this book and taking up the weapons the Lord has given us, you will have overcome and the enemy and these severe temptations will be a thing of the past as you rest in the Holy Spirit's mercy to keep you pure. *(1 John 5:18)* Sweet FREEDOM. It's coming...

Sins of Omission

We commit sins of omission when we know the right thing to do and do not do it. This is why a half truth is still considered a lie and therefore a sin, this is why laziness is warned against in Proverbs. These are sneaky passive sins and over time, if we ignore the Holy Spirit's prompting to repent (retire and return), these sins open the same doors to the enemy that the sins of commission opened. Even prayerlessness is sin according to Samuel! *(1 Samuel 12:23)* Half truths, laziness and prayerlessness among other passive sins are characteristics of Satan, and the goal is nothing in common, remember? Psalm 139:23-24 is our saving grace, it is the catapult to repentance and its resulting victory. Pray it and listen for the Lord's response often.

Generational Sins

Throughout the bible we see men of God like Moses, Ezra, Nehemiah, Jeremiah, Daniel and more repenting on behalf of their people. (In their cases, the people of Israel.) This form of repentance did not wipe the past offenders clean, but it did break off the sin effects from the person repenting and invite God to come and work on behalf of the nation. God follows His own laws, and therefore in order for Him to intervene after people choose Satan, somebody has to repent, somebody has to declare that they are returning to Him and His ways, God says those someones are 'His people'. *(2 Chronicles 7:14)* That's us.

> *"The LORD is slow to anger and abounding in steadfast love, forgiving iniquity (perversity/depravity) and transgression, (rebellion) but he will by no means clear the guilty, visiting the iniquity of the fathers on the children, to the third and the fourth generation."*
>
> *(Numbers 14:18 ESV)*

The evil acts are passed down to us through the blood of our father. Jesus was the only sinless man ever born after Adam's original sin because Jesus has no earthly father.

Here is further scientific explanation by Martin R. DeHaan, M.D, *"It is now definitely known that the blood which flows in an unborn babies arteries and veins is not derived from the mother but is produced within the body of the fetus itself only after the introduction of the male sperm. An unfertilized ovum can never develop blood since the female egg does not by itself contain the elements essential for the production of this blood. It is only after the male element has entered the ovum that blood can develop."*

This then seems to indicate the need to only confess and repent of the sins of the father, however, knowing that the Lord is welcomed to act after repentance, *(2 Chronicles 7:14)* I recommend standing in the gap for our mother's side of the family as well.

When I prayed Psalm 139:23-24 for myself asking God to reveal to me the wicked ways that were in me specifically from generations before, it was as if a crystal clear movie started playing in front of my eyes, each sin act would play over until I understood it and said it out loud in repentance, then the next scene would start. I saw everything from murder and greed to gossip and gambling, but the most heartbreaking was a scene of two people inside a house on a city street, slamming the door in the face of those in need. It was antisemitism. I burst into tears at the realization that this had any part in my family's past and therefore, in me. I repented and immediately the Lord reminded me of how just a few months prior to this prayer, I had walked the streets of Israel praying for His blessing on the people there. In His magnificent grace, He allowed me to make restitution in my heart before I even knew that I needed to. Talk about FREEDOM! What an amazing God we serve! And what a blessing to be the one to stand up in repentance and change the legacy of our family forevermore. You have this same opportunity. Let's go...

Prayers of Repentance

I learned through the Bethel Sozo inner healing and deliverance training the benefits of tackling repentance by breaking down our sinful acts into categories. The bible doesn't say we need to do this, but it is a wonderful way to address every area without forgetting anything. And if we are carrying demons, they are sometimes identified by type which coincide with the sin categories. So once we repent of all sins in that category and forgive those involved-their legal right is removed and we can kick them out. (More on forgiveness and deliverance in later chapters.) You do not have to use these or even go in any particular order but should you choose to do so, your Psalm 139 prayer would sound something like this, *"Search me, O God, and know my heart: try me, and know my thoughts: And see if there be any wicked way in me in the area of _____, and lead me in the way everlasting. In Jesus's righteous name, Amen."*

The sin categories that have come up while ministering with the Lord to myself and others are-

Sins of FEAR

Sins of SEXUALITY

Sins of ANGER

Sins of THE OCCULT and ADDICTION

Sins of CRIME and REBELLION

Sins of APATHY and COMPLACENCY

Listen to His answers one by one in each area then pray something similar to the prayer below for everything He reveals, trust the Holy Spirit to lead you using your own words and scriptures as you pray. This is not a ritual but rather time spent with the Lord who loves you.

It's important to note that you must trust that the Lord is speaking. I could write a whole book just on hearing the voice of the Lord, but for now, I urge you to trust by faith that if you pray this scripture to Him for the sake of repentance and walking in His ways, He will answer immediately. He speaks through pictures, sounds, memories, movie like scenes, words spelled out, song lyrics, smells, feelings and more. Pray His word, then pay attention to what happens next-whatever it is, that is His first answer in response to you asking Him to search you.

Even if what you 'hear' through any of the means listed above seems totally off, trust it is Him, and if you don't understand ask Him to explain. Here are three examples of times that it seemed like what I was seeing (I 'hear' the Lord mostly in pictures) was nothing but ended up being very significant.

The first I was praying for a woman and saw a man with an ax in the back of his head. I actually tried to rebuke it and silently confessed the violent thoughts. Only as the picture persisted did I realize that it was the Lord. I spoke it to the woman who then broke down in tears in confession and repentance for tearing somebody down behind their back about their lack of intelligence. Her words were actually cursing the person's mind.

The second, was for myself, I saw a dill pickle and had no idea why or what it could possibly mean. It surely couldn't mean something spiritual right? Wrong. Ends up it unfolded a story from my childhood (that had nothing to do with actual dill pickles!) that caused me an emotional wound. I forgave the person and got healing that I didn't even know I needed. God knew, He wants the deepest parts of us clean and free. You can trust Him.

The third was during a freedom session with a friend, we were going through the occult sin area and I saw a long, ancient piece of carved wood. It had divots that were filled with little pebbles. As I told her what I was seeing her eyes got huge and she jumped up to pull a Mancala board from storage under the tv stand. It was a modern version of what I had seen in prayer. We did some research and ends up that at its invention, Mancala was most likely used for occultic rituals. Who knew right? This is why it is important to let the Lord lead us in the

Psalm 139 prayer, there are things that we do not even know that we need to repent of that the enemy can use to keep strongholds in our lives. So let's get to repenting....

For Personal Sins-Thank you Father for searching out the wicked ways within me and leading me into Your ways everlasting. Thank you for Your grace in giving me the ability to repent and be holy merely by confession of my sins and belief in the justification of the cross Jesus. Today I stand before you and confess the sins of (list the sins that He shows you, not the categories, one by one.) I admit to rebelling against You in committing these evil acts and today I retire from them forever and return back to You and Your ways forevermore. I ask You to forgive me, in Jesus's name and I gladly receive Your forgiveness and gracious washing of all wickedness, transgressions and iniquities from my body, soul and spirit. I declare right now that I break any agreements that I have made with Satan or his demons as a son or daughter of darkness in committing these sins, and I sever his legal right to my life as I proclaim that I am now and forevermore an eternal child of light in the almighty name of Jesus. I now lay aside the deeds of darkness and put on the armor of light. Thank you, Merciful Father. Amen. *(Psalm 139:23-24, 1 John 1:9, Romans 10:9-11, Psalm 51:2, Ephesians 5:8, Romans 13:12)*

For Generational Sins-Thank you Father that you have promised that as humble myself, pray, turn to and search for You, You will hear from heaven and come and heal my land. (people) I stand in repentance for myself and my family and confess the sins of (list the sins that He shows you, not the categories, one by one.) Forgive me Father, cleanse me and my family line from here on out with the shed blood of Jesus Christ for our justification forevermore. I declare that we will no longer walk as sons and daughters of darkness, but as children of light according to your word, and I ask that you will sever the consequences of the sins of my fathers off of me and my generations for all eternity and that great will be our peace as You teach us to walk in Your ways. I receive Your forgiveness and choose to leave a righteous inheritance of serving You, Lord, to my children for generation upon generation. In Jesus's name. Amen. *(2 Chronicles 7:14, Romans 10:9-11, Isaiah 54:13, 17, Proverbs 13:22)*

Weapon Three:

The Three Baptisms

I baptize you with water, for repentance, but the one coming after me is more powerful than I am -- I am not worthy to carry his sandals. He will baptize you with the Holy Spirit and fire.

(Matthew 3:11 NET)

When we hear the word baptism most of us think of water and even then, have very little understanding of what it truly means, but there is so much more. To be truly forever free in our walk with Jesus, each of us must embrace by faith-water, Holy Spirit and fire baptism.

Baptism with Water

In baptism we show that we have been saved from death and doom by the resurrection of Christ; not because our bodies are washed clean by the water but because in being baptized we are turning to God and asking him to cleanse our hearts from sin. *(1 Peter 3:21)*

There has been much debate about whether we need to be baptized with water to be 'saved'. The answer is no...and yes. The word for 'save' in the original language of Greek is *sózó*, and once we understand the depth of meaning packed into this little word we realize that saying a prayer just to get to heaven was never God's intention. Salvation involves so much more. We know that not being baptized does not keep us out of heaven because Jesus told the thief on the cross that he would be with Him in paradise that very day when they were being crucified *(Luke 23:43)*, but digging deeper we find that the word gives major implications of what this life here should look like.

Sózó -to save, keep safe and sound, to rescue from danger or destruction, to save a suffering one (from perishing), i.e. one suffering from disease, to make well, heal, restore to health, to preserve one who is in danger of destruction, to save or rescue, to save in the technical biblical sense to save from the evils which obstruct the reception of the Messianic deliverance...(blueletterbible.com)

AMAZING. So, do we need to be water baptized in order to go to heaven? No. Do we need to be water baptized in order to embrace freedom? YES, absolutely, yes. Whoever believes and is baptized will be saved, (*sózó* – rescued, kept safe and sound, made well, restored to health, kept from suffering and destruction!) but whoever does not believe will be condemned. *(Mark 16:16)*

The Old Testament Pictures of Water Baptism

There are at least two pictures of water baptism in the Old Testament that I want to talk about briefly, remembering that everything in the Old Testament is a spiritual foreshadowing of what's to come in Jesus. I say 'at least' because knowing our awesome and mysterious God, there are probably more examples of water baptism that I have yet to discover!

The first is the Exodus of God's people...

"And the children of Israel shall go on dry ground through the midst of the sea."

(Exodus 14:16 NKJV)

You know the story, the Lord sent Moses to deliver the people from their slavery in Egypt under the rule of Pharaoh. He sent plague after plague and Pharaoh finally agreed to let God's people go, only to then send his army to hunt them down while they were in the wilderness. This sounds much like our salvation story. Pharaoh is the Satan-figure who has God's people bound in slavery and even though the all-powerful God has delivered them through the Christ-figure, Moses, Satan and his army with their ever-hardening hearts pursue and try to once again establish authority and rule over God's people, the Israelites. The most interesting part of this story is that final deliverance from their pre-salvation life came from passing through the midst of the sea. Their enemies were drowned behind them as they pressed on after their savior in faith while passing through the waters. Everyone went into the sea, but only God's people were brought out to live while their enemies died behind them. This is a picture of death and resurrection to new life. Because this OT story is a supernatural picture of escaping 'death' as God's people pass through water, could it mean that water baptism is meant as a supernatural means of delivering us from our enemy along with the vows and demonic oppression that he has us under? Yes, I think absolutely yes! Let's keep going.

Our next OT example is Noah... The Lord saw that the wickedness of man was great in the earth, and that every intention of the thoughts of his heart was only evil continually...

"But Noah found favor in the eyes of the Lord."

(Genesis 6:5, 8 ESV)

As we see earlier in this chapter, the reason that the wickedness of man was great on the earth is because a demonic breed of angels called Nephilim had laid with human women and created a hybrid breed of half demon/half human beings. (If you would like to learn more about the Nephilim, Chuck Missler of Koinonia House has many great teachings on the subject.) And as you know, God's plan to deal with the evil was water, again.

According to verse 9, Noah was righteous. As such he was chosen as a savior figure to rescue others by partnering with the Lord. By faith Noah made a way that would allow him and his family to pass through the fatal flood waters in resurrection while all evil mankind drown to permanent death in the water. Are we seeing a pattern here? Could it be that one purpose of water baptism is to deliver us from the evil that has been seeking to destroy us and our righteousness? I believe it the answer is YES.

Jesus's Baptism

When John tried to refuse to baptize Jesus, stating that it should be the other way around, Jesus replied,

"Let it be so now, for thus it is fitting for us to fulfill all righteousness."(Matthew 3:15 ESV) "...to fulfill all righteousness..."

That is interesting. To fulfill all righteousness the Jews had to be liberated from Eqypt, in order to do that they had to follow the 'savior' Moses, in faith, through the water. To fulfill all righteousness the human race had to be delivered from the demonic breed of hybrids that was threatening to take over the earth, once again they had to follow a 'savior', this time Noah, in faith, through the water. And in order to fulfill all righteousness now, we must follow Jesus, THE SAVIOR, in faith, through the water. This is God's plan for full righteousness. What is righteousness? From the Greek, *dikaiosynē*, as stated in this verse, it means in a broad sense: state of him who is as he ought to be. In order for us to be as we ought to be, we must go through the water after our Savior Jesus.

Since I have not heard anyone else teach on this* and am discovering this pattern as I seek the Lord in the scriptures to teach me more about baptism for the purpose of writing this book, I have not had the chance to test out what He is showing me. Further, since I did not have the faith at the time of my own baptisms, this particular purpose of water baptism was not fully activated in my life. (According to scripture as a whole, everything the Lord does in and through us is activated by FAITH. *(see Hebrews 11)*) Since our Lord is outside of time I can activate this purpose now through declaration, and you can do the same. If you feel after reading this you would like to be water baptized again, there is no reason at all that you cannot. If you feel the Holy Spirit prompting you to do that, then do not wait!

I had the opportunity on a trip to Israel to be baptized a second time in the Jordan River like Jesus, so of course I jumped at it! Both baptisms were significant turning points in my life. Not too long after my first water baptism in a jacuzzi at my church in 2000, the power of the Holy Spirit came on me and my whole life was changed forever. Then during my baptism in the Jordan River in 2015, Tom Jones of Global Awakening prophesied over me just before submerging, *"Lord, some are called and some are commissioned, let this be a commissioning, let this one be commissioned."* I didn't even know what he meant at the time but something in me broke and I started sobbing and didn't stop for quite some time after. A couple of months later the Lord called me to take my own team to India on mission, and this year I am taking another team to France and on the very day that I am writing this, I was just asked to bring a team to Pakistan. Reaching the harvest and setting the captives free has taken on new meaning in my spirit ever since that day in the Jordan. I have forever been commissioned by the Lord. Yes, water baptism changes everything.

Faith Filled Prayer for Water Baptism

Heavenly Father, I choose You, through your Son Jesus Christ, thank you for saving me. Thank you for calling me out of darkness and into your magnificent light. I renounce all agreements, promises, vows and covenants that are between me and Satan, and me and any of his workers of evil. Each of these is broken in Jesus name as I choose to die to my old person and be buried and raised again with Jesus through the waters of baptism. Thank you for delivering me from my enemies that will be drowned in the water and buried with my old life as I, by faith, pass safely through with Jesus to my new life with You. Please fulfill Your righteousness in me as I follow my Savior Jesus through the death, burial and resurrection by Your Glory to eternal life and all the freedom, peace, joy, victory and other heavenly gifts that come with that, In Jesus's name, amen. (1 Peter 2:9, Psalm 18:48, Romans 6:4-11, Matthew 3:14-16)

Baptism with the Holy Spirit

"Did you receive the Holy Spirit when you believed?" They answered, "No, we have not even heard that there is a Holy Spirit."

(Acts 19:2 NIV)

My personal testimony, in a nutshell, is that I was 'saved' at a Baptist youth group retreat when I was fifteen years old. I was told at that time that Jesus lived in my heart and what I should and shouldn't do to be a good Christian, which I then unsuccessfully tried to accomplish. Fifteen years later I met a man who asked me if I had ever been baptized in the Holy Spirit to which I responded by telling him my baptism in the jacuzzi story, he then took me to the scripture above and my entire life changed forever.

You can hear the full testimony on my You Tube channel under the title 'Baptism of the Holy Spirit, my personal testimony.' For now, I want to talk a bit about the theology. We learn from John the Baptist in Matthew 3:11 and Luke 3:16 that it is JESUS that baptizes us with the Holy Spirit. And from Acts 19:2 (above) that someone can believe in and profess Jesus, then be waiting to be baptized in the Holy Spirit until someone tells them that there is such a thing, such was my case. Acts 19 goes onto tell us that these believers, about twelve men, said they were baptized into John's baptism in the name of Jesus (that's water baptism) and that when Paul laid hands on them in this moment the Holy Spirit came upon them and they spoke in tongues and prophesied. One minute they were living normal life as water baptized believers in Jesus, the next minute miracles were coming out of their mouth at the moment of the baptism of the Holy Spirit. We read a similar story in Acts 8:16-17 (For the Spirit had not yet come upon any of them, but they had only been baptized in the name of the Lord Jesus.)Then Peter and John placed their hands on the Samaritans, and they received the Holy Spirit. (NET)

Imagine what it would be like to hang out with Jesus, to go into the streets to feed the homeless, cast out demons and heal the sick with Him. Imagine what it would be like to sit and eat with Him and lay your head on His chest and listen to His heartbeat like John did. Then imagine BETTER.

> *"But in fact, it is best for you that I go away, because if I don't, the Advocate won't come. If I do go away, then I will send him to you.*
>
> *(John 16:7 NLT)*

This is Jesus talking to the disciples saying it is better if He goes away because then He can send them the gift of the Holy Spirit. I hear people say all the time that they wish they could have walked with Jesus, but according to Him, He gives us something even better. The Advocate, Helper, Comforter...the Holy Spirit.

> *"But you will receive power when the Holy Spirit comes upon you. And you will be my witnesses, telling people about me everywhere--in Jerusalem, throughout Judea, in Samaria, and to the ends of the earth."*
>
> *Acts 1:8*

This is Jesus talking, when the Holy Spirit comes on us, we receive POWER. Here is an outline of biblical use of the Greek word for power (dynamis) in the bible from Blue Letter Bible- strength power, ability

1. inherent power, power residing in a thing by virtue of its nature, or which a person or thing exerts and puts forth
2. power for performing miracles
3. moral power and excellence of soul
4. the power and influence which belong to riches and wealth
5. power and resources arising from numbers
6. power consisting in or resting upon armies, forces, hosts

And no I did not forget a comma between strength and power; That IS the definition, 'strength power'! And who did Jesus say takes back the kingdom? The violent or STRONG. And how do we take it back? By force or POWER.

As you can see, the key to unlocking all other means of overcoming the enemy and living victoriously in this life, is the baptism in the Holy Spirit. That is where our power to live comes from. There is no other source.

When the Holy Spirit came upon me for the first time I woke up with biblical knowledge flowing through me that I had never had before. I could quote scripture, in context, with wisdom, that I had never heard nor read! That was sixteen years ago and the Holy Spirit still flows through me in that way. It is miraculous!!!! I was called a walking encyclopedia the other day. So funny! I was a C student at best and failed history twice. I'm not kidding, and now I'm being called a walking encyclopedia as the bible flows out of my mouth, that is the power of the Holy Spirit.

Two days after that first powerful moment I was speaking in tongues and now can go back and forth between two heavenly languages depending on what the Holy Spirit is trying to accomplish through me in the moment. Dreaming and interpretation is an almost daily occurrence, compassion and love flow in spite of me, casting out demons is second nature, prophecy comes almost as naturally as breathing and my team and I recently saw food multiplied for a village of two hundred to have enough to take communion! This is not me, this is the power of the baptism of the Holy Spirit. Although He always perfectly reflects His true character found in the pages of scripture, He looks different flowing through each one of us. One needs only to read the four gospels to see that!

But I Thought I Received The Holy Spirit at Salvation?

"In him you also, when you heard the word of truth, the gospel of your salvation, and believed in him, were sealed with the promised Holy Spirit, who is the guaranteed of our inheritance until we acquire possession of it, to the praise of his glory."

(Ephesians 1:13-14 ESV)

Yes, you did, sort of. Your spirit is what will live on in eternity and according to the scripture above when you heard and believed it was sealed with the Holy Spirit as guarantee of your heavenly inheritance until you are in possession of it. But that is your spirit, so what about the rest of you?

"For this reason I bow my knees before the Father, from whom every family in heaven and on earth is named, that according to the riches of his glory he may grant you to be strengthened with power through his Spirit in your inner being, so that Christ may dwell in your hearts through faith—that you, being rooted and grounded in love, may have strength to comprehend with all the saints what is the breadth and length and height and depth, and to know the love of Christ that surpasses knowledge, that you may be filled with all the fullness of God."

(Ephesians 3:14-19 ESV)

This is one of my favorite scripture prayers for my husband and girls, it is taped to my bathroom mirror for me to declare for them as I get ready each morning. My whole family was sealed with the Holy Spirit as each of them accepted Jesus as Savior in their youth, but oh for each of them to be strengthened with power in their inner being (spirit), that Christ would dwell in their hearts (spirit/soul/emotions), that they would have the strength to comprehend (mind) all the spiritual dimensions of Christ's love, that they would be filled with all the fullness of God in their spirits, souls and bodies!

The best and simplest theology that I have heard on the Baptism of the Holy Spirit is by David Hernandez of David Hernandez Ministries. He explained that the Baptism of the Spirit is not us getting more of God, but God getting more of us. It is the moment when the Holy Spirit who has sealed our spirit is asked to come and FLOOD all the rest of us. It is when the Holy Spirit is invited to take over our whole spirit, soul and body and flow up, throughout and forward to minister to ourselves and others. So amazing.

"He who believes in Me, as the Scripture said, 'From his innermost being will flow rivers of living water.'"

(John 7:38 NASB)

The baptism of the Holy Spirit then, is a living water flood that overtakes us...it's full immersion to the point of overflow.

So, what will the Holy Spirit do as He flows through you? Only He knows...If you have been following the steps through salvation, repenting, washing in the water and have surrendered your life fully to Jesus then He wants to give you the gift of the Holy Spirit, just ask and by faith and receive.

"...If you then, though you are evil, know how to give good gifts to your children, how much more will your Father in heaven give the Holy Spirit to those who ask him!"

(Luke 11:13 NIV)

Baptism with Fire

"He will baptize you with the Holy Spirit and fire."

(Matthew 3:11 NET)

I have gone back and forth in prayer about whether to include the Baptism of Fire in this book, there is so much debate about what it even means that how can I possibly think I can address it here? Well, I believe I must try because it is my understanding that we can never be fully free without it, and now am excited to do so as the Lord has given me new understanding even as I write. He is so good.

Again, looking to an Old Testament example of a baptism of fire we see the incredible story of Shaddrach, Meshach and Abednego. I thought about just pulling a verse here or there but the whole story is so incredible and significant that I decided to include the whole thing. I ask that before I continue with the revelation of the Lord regarding the baptism of fire, that you read this account from Daniel 3 with new eyes, it is truly extraordinary.

> *"Nebuchadnezzar the king made an image of gold, whose height was sixty cubits, and its width six cubits: he set it up in the plain of Dura, in the province of Babylon. 2 Then Nebuchadnezzar the king sent to gather together the satraps, the deputies, and the governors, the judges, the treasurers, the counselors, the sheriffs, and all the rulers of the provinces, to come to the dedication of the image which Nebuchadnezzar the king had set up. 3 Then the satraps, the deputies, and the governors, the judges, the treasurers, the counselors, the sheriffs, and all the rulers of the provinces, were gathered together to the dedication of the image that Nebuchadnezzar the king had set up; and they stood before the image that Nebuchadnezzar had set up. 4 Then the herald cried aloud, To you it is commanded, peoples, nations, and languages, 5 that whenever you hear the sound of the horn, flute, zither, lyre, harp, pipe, and all kinds of music, you fall down and worship the golden image that Nebuchadnezzar the king has set up; 6 and whoever doesn't fall down and worship shall the same hour be cast into the middle of a burning fiery furnace. 7 Therefore at that time, when all the peoples heard the sound of the horn, flute, zither, lyre, harp, pipe, and all kinds of music, all the peoples, the nations, and the languages, fell down and worshiped the golden image that Nebuchadnezzar the king had set up. 8 Therefore at that time certain Chaldeans came near, and brought accusation against the Jews. 9 They answered Nebuchadnezzar the king, O king, live for ever. 10 You, O king, have made a decree, that every man that shall hear the sound of the horn, flute, zither, lyre, harp, pipe, and all kinds of music, shall fall down and worship the golden image; 11 and whoever doesn't fall down*

and worship shall be cast into the middle of a burning fiery furnace. 12 There are certain Jews whom you have appointed over the affairs of the province of Babylon: Shadrach, Meshach, and Abednego; these men, O king, have not respected you. They don't serve your gods, nor worship the golden image which you have set up. 13 Then Nebuchadnezzar in rage and fury commanded to bring Shadrach, Meshach, and Abednego. Then they brought these men before the king. 14 Nebuchadnezzar answered them, Is it on purpose, Shadrach, Meshach, and Abednego, that you don't serve my god, nor worship the golden image which I have set up? 15 Now if you are ready whenever you hear the sound of the horn, flute, zither, lyre, harp, pipe, and all kinds of music to fall down and worship the image which I have made, good: but if you don't worship, you shall be cast the same hour into the middle of a burning fiery furnace; and who is that god that shall deliver you out of my hands? 16 Shadrach, Meshach, and Abednego answered the king, Nebuchadnezzar, we have no need to answer you in this matter. 17 If it happens, our God whom we serve is able to deliver us from the burning fiery furnace; and he will deliver us out of your hand, O king. 18 But if not, let it be known to you, O king, that we will not serve your gods, nor worship the golden image which you have set up. 19 Then was Nebuchadnezzar full of fury, and the form of his appearance was changed against Shadrach, Meshach, and Abednego. He spoke, and commanded that they should heat the furnace seven times more than it was usually heated. 20 He commanded certain mighty men who were in his army to bind Shadrach, Meshach, and Abednego, and to cast them into the burning fiery furnace. 21 Then these men were bound in their pants, their tunics, and their mantles, and their other clothes, and were cast into the middle of the burning fiery furnace. 22 Therefore because the king's commandment was urgent, and the furnace exceeding hot, the flame of the fire killed those men who took up Shadrach, Meshach, and Abednego. 23 These three men, Shadrach, Meshach, and Abednego, fell down bound into the middle of the burning fiery furnace. 24 Then Nebuchadnezzar the king was astonished, and rose up in haste: he spoke and said to his counselors, Didn't we cast three men bound into the middle of the fire? They answered the king, True, O king. 25 He answered, Look, I see four men loose, walking in the middle of the fire, and they are unharmed; and the aspect of the fourth is like a son of the gods. 26 Then Nebuchadnezzar came near to the mouth of the burning fiery

> *furnace: he spoke and said, Shadrach, Meshach, and Abednego, you servants of the Most High God, come out, and come here. Then Shadrach, Meshach, and Abednego came out of the middle of the fire. 27 The satraps, the deputies, and the governors, and the king's counselors, being gathered together, saw these men, that the fire had no power on their bodies, nor was the hair of their head singed, neither were their pants changed, nor had the smell of fire passed on them. 28 Nebuchadnezzar spoke and said, Blessed be the God of Shadrach, Meshach, and Abednego, who has sent his angel, and delivered his servants who trusted in him, and have changed the king's word, and have yielded their bodies, that they might not serve nor worship any god, except their own God. 29 Therefore I make a decree, that every people, nation, and language, which speak anything evil against the God of Shadrach, Meshach, and Abednego, shall be cut in pieces, and their houses shall be made a dunghill; because there is no other god who is able to deliver after this sort. 30 Then the king promoted Shadrach, Meshach, and Abednego in the province of Babylon.*
>
> (WEB)

Praise God this is MAGNIFICENT! We know that 'baptism' describes full immersion, exactly like Shadrach, Meshach and Abednego experienced in the fiery furnace. In Matthew 3:11 quoted at the top of this section, John specifically referred to power in regards to the types of baptism that Jesus would do. Man can light a match, man can persecute, man can throw someone into a fire, John could have done any number of things with fire, but it takes supernatural power to protect someone in the midst of it. John couldn't baptize in the Holy Spirit and John couldn't baptize in fire. It is this author's belief that the baptism of fire from Jesus that John spoke of, is the power to stand in the face of persecution for our faith, the protection within the punishment, not the punishment itself, and the promotion that comes having been immersed in fire and survived unscathed.

If this truly is an Old Testament account of the baptism of fire, then this baptism cannot be referring to God testing us with suffering as many believe. God did not light the fire, the king, inspired by pride and ego (that has Satan's name written all over it) ordered it. And Shaddrach, Meshach and Abednego did not suffer. Quite the opposite- they didn't even smell like fire and not even their hair was singed! No, the baptism of fire is something else entirely.

Kings Protecting Their Crowns

The story starts with King Nebuchadnezzar erecting an idol for all to worship in the plain of Dura, in the province of Babylon. It is interesting to note that the name Nebuchadnezzar means, 'may Nebo protect the crown', Dura means 'dwelling', and Babylon means 'confusion by mixing'.

Up until the point of surrender to Jesus as King, we all serve other kings, idol kings. Some serve themselves, others serve their spouse, children, their job, money, addictions, gods of false religions (Hinduism, New Age, Buddhism, Mormonism, etc.) It is no coincidence that the antagonist in the OT account of the baptism of fire was given a name that shows a false king protecting his crown. When you come to Jesus, the enemy will try to protect his place as king of your life by getting you to continue in the worship of idols, the more things vying for your worship, the better chance he has of hanging onto his crown as king of your life. He tries to confuse your allegiance to Jesus by mixing in as many other options as he can think of. The tendency is to think that only people in India, Africa or the like need to worry about false worship of idols, but don't be fooled, Satan erects idols of many forms, wherever our dwelling.

Persecution

The consequence of our brave trio refusing to worship anyone but the Lord was a literal baptism of fire. They were willing to refuse the king and stand up for the one true God even if He did not rescue them. (vs 17-18) The king was so enraged that he ordered that the fire be turned up seven times hotter, don't be surprised if the more you sing praises to Jesus and remain loyal to Him, the more the enemy turns up the heat. Also, do not be surprised if the fire comes through the people around you.

If you read the whole story then you know that Shaddrach, Meshach and Abednego were thrown into the fiery furnace only to be protected by the One they worship. Just as the baptism of the Holy Spirit is a gift, the baptism of fire is a gift. God did not put the three men in the fire, the earthly king did, God's gift, the baptism of fire, was the supernatural protection and encounter that came once man threw them in. All the way up to that point, they had a choice, and so do we. I do not believe that God throws us into the fire, it is a choice to stand, stand, stand in the face of accusations, threat of personal harm, and even death. It is our choice to have the faith to say, *"He is able to deliver us, but even if he doesn't, we still will not worship any other god."* Then it is the enemy's hand that throws us into the fire, and it is God's hand that brings us out.

Promotion & Praises

What happens when we stand our ground and refuse to cave in the face of temptation and false worship? We are protected, then promoted, and others -maybe even our human persecutors- will see that the God we serve is the One True King and they too will worship Him. (vs 29-30)

Your Personal Persecution

I can't tell you how this will play out in your life, most likely the enemy will attack where he has the best chance of getting you to cave. My baptism of fire came just a few weeks after I was baptized with the power of the Holy Spirit when a knock at my door resulted in court papers that I was once again being sued for custody of my middle daughter by her unbelieving dad.

The first case 3 years earlier was relatively peaceful, this second one turned into an on again off again eleven-year battle where my faith was used as evidence against me in accusation that I was mentally ill among other things. I was called a religious zealot (I will take that as a compliment, thank you!), I was accused of neglect and abuse, of withholding visitation, of purposely having children so I could collect child support (which I was not even collecting), and so much more. I legally had to let my baby girl spend weeks at a time with people who were on a mission to make her hate me as they did. Many times, they wouldn't even let her speak to me on the phone during her long summer visits as a toddler. I have tears now writing about it. I was stalked with video cameras everywhere I went for months at a time, dragged into DCFS for questioning, confronted by police on a weekly basis, and spent more time in the courtroom that any one person should ever have to. I was unable to protect my daughter from the custody battle trauma and attempts at alienation that had become the overarching theme of her young life. I was exhausted and had prayed for so long that I had nothing left to pray.

After one especially disheartening day in court where no one seemed to notice or care that my daughter was being used as a tool for her dad and his family to exercise their hatred toward me, I walked out with tears streaming down my face into the crowded third floor family court hallway looked up and said, *"Where are You? Jesus, where are You?"* I then looked at my mom with the same hopeless plea, *"Where is He?"*

Right then an elevator door opened and about a dozen people poured out into the already packed hallway. Our eyes all fixed on a man with shoulder length brown hair, beautifully compassionate eyes, and a mustache...you guessed it, he looked exactly like all the depictions of Jesus I had ever seen, even down to being dressed in plain white from the waist up.

He set his eyes directly on me and proceeded to walk in my direction in spite of the hundred-other people in the hall. He got so close to me that I opened my mouth to speak, (I was so stunned that I seriously have no idea what I would've even said), then he veered and circled around us and proceeded to walk back the way he came, onto the elevator and we never saw him again. I stood there stunned, silent, with my mouth hanging open in awe. There He was. He walked into my fire with me just as He had Shadrach, Meshach and Abednego. Was it really Jesus? Honestly I am not sure. It was probably just a man that got off on the wrong floor of the courthouse that day. But I knew, it was the Lord's answer to my cry to heaven, *"Jesus, where are you?"*

The fire was not pleasant, it was heartbreaking on so many levels. But we were protected. I kept my custody again and again as the many judges ruled in my favor against all odds. Today at 20 years old, my daughter is happy, healthy and amazing in spite of what we went through.

The False Fire

Many times in scripture we see references to people passing their children through the fire in satanic rituals of sacrifice to Molech, Baal and other demons. *(Leviticus18:21-3, 20:2-5, Deuteronomy 12:31, 18:10, 2 Kings 17:17, Psalm 106:37-38, Jeremiah 32:35.)* It is the enemy's horrific way of imitating the beautiful gift of the baptism of fire from our Heavenly Father. In working with survivors of Satanic Ritual Abuse, I have learned that everything good God has ordained for His children, Satan creates a counterfeit ritual in the natural so that we mistrust our Lord. He either actually recreates these things using children and adult victims in rituals at the hands of his servants, or he twists the meaning of the scriptures to reflect false ideas of what the Lord meant. In this case the way he has twisted the baptism of fire is to make people believe that God hurts them to make them stronger, better, love Him more, etc. When the truth is, Jesus told us that in this world we would have trouble yes, *(John 16:33)* but He also tells us that He does not willingly cause grief. *(Lamentations 3:33)* Discipline, yes, as a loving parent disciplines a child when the need arises, but grief, no.

Be assured, the baptism of fire is a wonderful thing. When the time comes that you need to defend your faith in Jesus, stand determined and unmoving, praise His name and works all the louder and watch and see what He will do!

WEAPON FOUR:

FORGIVENESS

For if you forgive men their trespasses, your Heavenly Father will also forgive you. But if you do not forgive men their trespasses, neither will your Father forgive yours.

(Matthew 6:15 BSB)

    Forgiveness...What is it? From the Greek *aphiēmi*, it simply means- 'to let go', the root word from which it is derived, apo, actually means, 'a state of separation, distance.' Spiritually speaking when we forgive someone we are rightfully letting the person go and choosing to separate ourselves by leaving the offense behind us. We make a choice to give God room to work and judge in His perfect righteousness by taking ourselves out of the way through forgiveness. Romans 12:19 actually says we are to leave room for God's wrath and that He will repay! WOW. For those of us who have been the victim of a serious offense such as abuse or worse, this scripture is deeply comforting. There will be justice. However, while it is God's job to repay and bring justice, the scripture goes on in verse 20 to tell us that our role as the forgiver is to give food and drink to our enemies! Evidently leaving room for God doesn't mean just walking away, it means somehow loving them in the moment, but before we dive into that let's talk about what forgiveness is NOT.

What Forgiveness is NOT

Forgiveness is not trust nor the removal of boundaries, it is not approval nor a free pass, it is not surrender to the offender nor is it vulnerability before them. In fact, forgiveness, for the most part, is an exchange between you and the Lord, not between you and the person who hurt you.

Forgiveness is not a feeling or emotion. Forgiveness is a choice and action of our will. Unforgiveness is not a feeling either, what is happening in your soul when you feel bitter against somebody is an offshoot of ANGER. And what does the word say about anger?

"Be angry, yet do not sin."

(Ephesians 4:26 BSB)

Anger can actually be righteous. We should be angry when people hurt others through sin. So then, since anger is not a sin the feeling of unforgiveness in not a sin either. It is our reaction, or, the way we choose to act when we are angry, that is the key to either being bound in prison through the sin of unforgiveness or living free through a confession of forgiveness before the Lord. Our emotions are really irrelevant to forgiveness. Feelings indicate the need for some inner healing work with the Lord, but they are not an indicator of whether or not we can or have forgiven someone. This will make even more sense later in this chapter as I explain exactly how to forgive someone.

Supernatural Forgiveness

One of my favorite moments in this freedom ministry was when I was working with a survivor of Satanic Ritual Abuse and the Father gave me revelation about the familiar scripture from Psalm 23 verse 5...

"You prepare a table before me in the presence of my enemies;"

I always read this to mean that there would be some kind of vindication in front of the people who hurt us. That we would be lifted up by the King of Kings into a place of honor while our enemies watched on. I guess that's a tiny part, but not for the reason that I thought. Let me explain...

In our previous sessions this woman, I'll call her Emma, had made such huge strides to the point of being set free from a life long battle with anorexia. Her mind was being renewed and she was transforming with Jesus right before our eyes. Just by looking at her, her friends were asking her what had changed within a day of our first meeting! JESUS is AMAZING! But even with all the victories, Satan kept assaulting Emma with flashbacks of her abuse and each time she would find herself stricken with terror and unable to escape. After about three such episodes over a couple of months' time I started seeking the Lord for bigger answers. Something wasn't right. We knew she was free, we saw the fruit and the new person she was, she was filled with hope and joy and on fire for Jesus and then all the sudden out of nowhere she would spiral downward! Why was victory so easily forsaken every time Satan showed up with new memories? Should she have to process each and every memory that had ever happened in order to be free? If that was the case, this could go on forever and that is NOT freedom. We should not have to live each day wondering when another flashback to our pain will cripple us again. That is not what Jesus died for. So I pressed in for answers and our faithful Father answered above and beyond what I thought possible. He opened up one of the deep mysteries in scripture and took us straight to Heaven with Him to experience another dimension of forgiveness. It was astounding and I am going to share it with you so you can experience it too.

When we combine Psalm 23:5, you prepare a table before in the presence of my enemies..., with Romans 12:20-21, On the contrary,

"If your enemy is hungry, feed him; if he is thirsty, give him a drink...." We find the scriptural key to final forgiveness. Think about it, how often will

we get the opportunity to offer food and drink in the natural to those who sin against us? Is God expecting you to invite all those who hurt you in the past out to lunch when you get saved? That would be silly. No, this is a supernatural exchange empowered by the Lord Himself.

This is what He instructed me to do as I prepared for a phone session later in the morning with Emma. He reminded me that we are seated in the heavenly realms with Jesus *(Ephesians 2:6)*, and as such have access to all His promises. All we have to do is ask. So, she asked Jesus to prepare a table before her in the presence of her enemies and He did, and what a beautiful table it was! Then even though she was frightened, we asked that her enemies be lined up before her and one by one she invited them to share with her at the table that Jesus had prepared. She was at the head with Him, she was the guest of honor, and as such it was up to her to decide who got to eat and drink and who didn't. Being obedient to the Lord's mandate to offer food and drink to her hungry & thirsty enemies, she invited every single one to dine with her in God's goodness. What a magnificent exchange!

Looking even deeper we understand that what she was really offering was JESUS, Jesus is what these evil men and women were hungry for, they just didn't know it!

> *"Jesus replied, "I am the bread of life. Whoever comes to me will never be hungry again. Whoever believes in me will never be thirsty."*
>
> *(John 6:35 NLT)*

When we choose to forgive and offer blessing to our enemies, we are offering them JESUS. If you can do this in the natural without removing necessary boundaries, by all means do so, but more importantly, let your spirit commune with Jesus in the heavenlies to enter into Psalm 23 supernaturally to feed those who have hurt you. By faith, something happens in the heavenlies in this exchange. Your faithfulness may change their eternity. When we have been hurt so terribly that it seems like our life has been stolen from us, thoughts of our enemies 'burning in hell' are comforting. I get it, but remember, there will be justice if we leave room for God's wrath through our forgiveness. God will get vengeance on the wicked, but oh the sweetest reward for us would be if our faithfulness to His word rescued someone from the clutches of Satan because we embraced the power of the cross to the point of offering our enemies the same JESUS that saved us.

Imagine the tears of joy we will experience in heaven when we see that it was our faith and this incredible supernatural exchange in Heaven with Jesus that led to the repentance and redemption of the worst of sinners! Ah! I can only imagine!

What Does Forgiveness Have to Do with Freedom?

Why does it matter so much? Remember in the Salvation chapter we talked about having nothing in common with Satan? Well, unforgiveness is a biggie. Satan is the accuser *(Revelation 12:10)* so when we accuse, whether with our mouth or in our heart, we are joining with Satan against someone. When we refuse to forgive we are leaving fellowship Heavenly Father who calls us and empowers us through Jesus, and we are choosing to partner with Satan in his accusations against someone instead. This is a one or the other choice, we cannot serve both God and Satan. *(Matthew 6:24)*

> *"Then his lord called him in, and said to him, 'You wicked servant! I forgave you all that debt, because you begged me. Shouldn't you also have had mercy on your fellow servant, even as I had mercy on you?' His lord was angry, and delivered him to the tormentors, until he should pay all that was due to him. So my heavenly Father will also do to you, if you don't each forgive your brother from your hearts for his misdeeds."*
>
> *(Matthew 18:32-35 WEB)*

Yikes. The message of this parable told by Jesus is crystal clear, if we do not forgive after having been forgiven, then we are handed over to the tormentors or jailers to be tortured as some translations state. The only way to then get out of the enemy's prison is to pay all of our debts. How do we pay all of our debts? JESUS. Jesus paid our debts when He died on the cross so to get out of prison we must return to Him and His covering by choosing to declare forgiveness toward those who sin against us in spite of our emotions.

Wouldn't it be so much better to never end up in spiritual jail through unforgiveness in the first place? YES. We can love our offenders in the moment through a declaration of forgiveness to the Father. Just like Jesus did on the cross when He said, *"Father, forgive them, for they know not what they do." (Luke 23:24 ESV)*

Notice this act of forgiveness took place between Jesus and the Father, not Jesus and His crucifiers. We should follow suit. By all means, if someone apologizes feel free to vocalize that you forgive them, like a spouse, child or co-worker for instance. Someone with whom you are doing life and need a clean slate to get back on track with, but do not think that forgiveness means that you always have to go tell the offender that you have forgiven them. This is unnecessary and even dangerous at times, and other times it may just hurt the persons feelings had they not known that they had done anything wrong to begin with.

How to Forgive

Since we know we are seated in the heavenlies *(Ephesians 2:6)*, and we are allowed to approach God's throne of grace with confidence (Hebrews 4:16), that is exactly what we are going to do. Close your eyes and with your spirit by faith see yourself approaching His throne of grace in the heavenlies. Then confess with your mouth any sin of unforgiveness that you have been harboring against anyone (including yourself!) and receive His forgiveness. Then ask the Holy Spirit to bring to mind who you need to forgive, and declare outloud in your own words a prayer statement of forgiveness. Here are examples of forgiveness declarations...

Toward others- Heavenly Father, I come before you and I bring state the name of the person, today I choose to forgive them according to your word.. I break my agreement of accusation against them that I have been sharing with Satan the accuser, *(Revelation 12:10)* and I return to share in grace and forgiveness with Jesus and to have my debts paid, *(Matthew 18:34)* believing that His cross is big enough to cover even the worst of sins, mine and theirs. I take my hands off of them and leave them here for you to judge with your perfect justice, to redeem according to Your will, and to bless with the same grace, mercy & love with which you have blessed me. Release me from any jailers that have been tormenting me and my emotions due to my unforgiveness *(Matthew 18: 34)*, and heal the soul wounds *(Psalm 23:3)* that their sins against me caused. Jesus, come carry away my griefs and sorrows *(Isaiah 53:4)* and make me glad as the place of your dwelling, with the River of Living Waters, the Holy Spirit. In Jesus's name amen!

Toward yourself- Heavenly Father, I come before you and ask your forgiveness for the pride of holding onto my sins and failures when

Your word says that You are faithful to forgive *(John 1:9)* when I confess. I ask your forgiveness for my lack unbelief in Your goodness and the power of the cross to cover my sins. Today I declare that I am forgiven because of Jesus! And as such, I lay down my pride that says that my standards are higher than Yours, and I humbly receive Your forgiveness and choose to forgive myself for all of my sins, mistakes, regrets and failures of the past. I break my agreement with the accuser, Satan, and choose to partner with Jesus in His forgiveness of me. Thank you that my sins are as far as the east is from the west *(Psalm 103:12)* and that I am washed clean of them forever! In Jesus's magnificent name, amen!

Toward God- Heavenly Father, I confess that I have wrongfully blamed You for the hardships in my life and that I have not studied to show myself approved when it comes to Your character and the authority that You gave me in warfare over the evil one. *(2 Timothy 2:15)* I have lost earthly battles and have held unforgiveness in my heart toward You as a result of my own failure to embrace the power of the cross. Please forgive me and help me to know You and Your word better so I can fully embrace Your love, walk out the understanding that Jesus came to give me life to the full, and recognize that it is the enemy that has been working to kill, steal and destroy me *(John 10:10)* so that I will never blame You again. You are gracious, righteous & compassionate *(Psalm 116:5)*, thank You for forgiving me. Today I break my agreement with Satan of accusation against You and return to perfect fellowship with You, through Jesus. *(Colossians 1:21-22)* I am forever grateful, Amen.

WEAPON FIVE:

INNER HEALING

"There is a river whose streams make glad the city of God, the holy place where the Most High dwells."

(Psalm 46:4 NIV)

    I will never forget the day the Lord revealed to me the incredible healing mystery of Psalm 46. I was invited into someone's home to minister freedom to a small group of women. I had been praying for the

Lord to accelerate healing and deliverance in my ministry and crying out for answers of what that would look like. I knew that He was calling me personally out of one on one ministry sessions, but I also knew that my call to set the captives free in Jesus was just beginning so I was trying to figure out exactly what He was asking me to do. He showed me group sessions and I stepped out in faith and started telling people that's what I was available for. The goal was to give people a taste of freedom, and help them see JESUS- knowing once they did they couldn't help but fall in love with Him- then send them out with a few tools and a new Holy Spirit fire that would cause them to finish their freedom walk with the Lord. It is working beautifully! He is so faithful!

The morning of that first group session as I was seeking Him in my quiet time for what He wanted me to talk about, He led me to search for more understanding of inner healing. It was early on in my deliverance ministry that I had learned how important inner- emotional healing is and it didn't take long before I realized that learning to minister inner healing would be a life long journey for me. The mysteries of the human soul & spirit and our connection with our Creator are magnificent and deeper than we could possibly uncover in just one lifetime.

My Wake Up Call to the Need for Inner Healing

After spending a very long night ministering to a young woman, let's call her Macy*, who was hearing voices, self-harming and suicidal, we finally got breakthrough. The demons were gone, Macy got relief and posted praise to Jesus for freedom on her Facebook wall the next morning. Victory! Or so we thought.... Just a day or two later Macy was worse off than before we made the demons leave. She was angry at her friend who had asked us to come help her, she was blaspheming God, spewing hatred for Christians, and unfortunately, now even more hopeless. The craziest part? Macy was a worship leader at her church. It made no sense to me. How could a Christian worship leader be this bound by Satan? And why are the demons back? The answer was actually quite simple. The abuses of her childhood were never healed. When Macy got 'saved' and devoted her life to Jesus, nobody ever helped her connect with Him in a way that would allow Him to heal her soul and spirit of the horrific pain she had endured throughout most of her youth and adolescence. She was wrought with demons of shame, anxiety, suicide, self-hate, unforgiveness, fear, anger and more, all because of WOUNDEDNESS. In our authority we were able to make the demons leave, and of course we asked that she be filled with the Holy Spirit so that the demons would not go get friends and come back and make her worse like Jesus warned *(see Matthew 12:45)*. But little did I know at the time that He cannot dwell where there is woundedness. The Lord wants to shine His light and bring health into the places of your soul and spirit that have been hurt and defiled by the darkness. He will never leave nor forsake you *(Hebrews 13:5)*, but He cannot reside inside a broken area of our being. He wills to bring healing and fill the space where wounds once were with His glorious love and joy, but in no way does He dwell in the unhealed, wounded areas of our soul and spirit. You must invite Him in like you would a trusted surgeon that treats your physical body, to supernaturally heal the wounds before He can take residence.

Offending the Holy Spirit

"And do not grieve the Holy Spirit of God, by whom you were sealed for the day of redemption. Let all bitterness and wrath and anger and clamor and slander be put away from you, along with all malice. Be kind to one another, tenderhearted, forgiving one another, as God in Christ forgave you."

(Ephesians 4:30-31)

It is surprising to learn the meaning of the Greek word for 'clamor' used in the passage above in regards to grieving the Holy Spirit. The word is *Kraugé*, and it means an outcry in tumult or grief. Its root word, *krazō*, profoundly means to cry or pray for vengeance.

This scripture tells us that when we receive salvation by faith we are sealed with the Holy Spirit as we discussed in the Baptism chapter. That's the good news. Then we are told not to grieve Him with bitterness, wrath, anger, clamor and slander. A deeper meaning of the word grieve used here, *(lypeō)* is 'to offend'. Understanding how we offend the Holy Spirit changes everything.

When we read bitterness, wrath, anger and slander most of us tend to believe that Paul is talking to mean spirited & violent people so the clamor word just gets lost in the mix and we move on. The rest of us are just ordinary folks who are pretty nice most of the time, right? But when we dig deeper into the word clamor we get a hint to understanding the mystery spoken here. Each of the sins listed- bitterness, wrath, anger, clamoring and slandering- are born out of pain and grief. All of them.

Do you know the definition of the word wrath? (*Thymos* in the original Greek). It means, anger forthwith boiling up and soon subsiding again. It is a passionate anger that rises up and then goes away....sounds like what happens when someone does something that 'triggers' us. When we are 'triggered' we have an exaggerated emotional response to someone or something because an old wound was just reopened and is flaring up causing us to react in passionate anger that will soon subside, hmmm. All too familiar. And I'll be the first to admit that I have slandered in the name of 'venting' about someone who has hurt me past or present, my guess is you have too.

This entire chapter of Ephesians from vs 17 on, as well as the next chapter, deals with living the righteous life in Christ. Putting off the old self and putting on the new. Putting away malice, (evil intentions and deeds), forgiving others, being kind, not giving into sexual immorality, not getting drunk etc. All of these sins flow out of woundedness. Macy, was caught in the cycle of numbing her pain with drinking and one night stands like so many others. Without her partnering with Jesus to heal her wounds and inviting the Holy Spirit to bring light & life where pain & death were once inflicted, her wounds were left gaped open and festering. The evil spirits that had been dwelling in her wounds were easily allowed to rush back in as she remained in agreement with the feelings and lies associated with the wounding.

You know the saying, *"Hurt people, hurt people."* In extreme cases we see evidence of this most often in child abuse cases. An abused child grows up to abuse children. Heartbreaking. But we also see this in many marriages and often in cases like Macy's. She was mostly hurting herself, but her loved ones as well as they watched her self-destruct. Hurt people, hurt people, and hurting people is SIN. Nothing in common with the enemy, remember? We cannot remain wounded and be filled to the full with the Holy Spirit. We must invite the Lord's healing.

Identity

Macy's identity when we met her that day was PAIN & SHAME, and although we made the demons leave and she met the Holy Spirit in a way she hadn't before, her personal identity when we left was still pain & shame because her wounds had not been healed.

My heart breaks that I had any part in this and at my naivety of jumping in over my head and agreeing to deliver someone when I barely knew what I was doing. I looked up to the Lord right then and said, *"I won't do it again Lord. Forgive me and give me tools to heal their wounds in Jesus or I quit. I won't do another deliverance until I have understanding of how to facilitate your healing of soul and spirit."*

He is faithful and answered by leading me to the tools from Bethel Sozo's inner healing and deliverance ministry training that I mentioned in an earlier chapter and I have been using what I learned through that training as a foundation for inner healing ministry ever since. But the Lord continues to teach and show me more with each knew Freedom Session. There is always more to learn. The first lesson, if we use ministry tools as a 'program' for inner healing, healing will never happen. We must approach the desire for freedom with a mindset that our ultimate goal is to connect to the One who Heals, our Savior, Jesus Christ. When we connect supernaturally with Jesus, He changes our identity as defined by the emotions of our past pain, to the beauty of our present and future with Him. We can then invite the Holy Spirit to dwell where once was only found pain and darkness. This is inner healing.

Connecting to the Healer

As I searched 'Christian Inner Healing' that morning before my freedom event, I came across a blog post that quoted Psalm 46. I do not even remember the blog address or anything she said in the article because as soon as I read Psalm 46 through the lens of 'inner healing' I was undone as His goodness and grace washed over me with pure, blissful revelation once again. Our God is just astonishing! I am going to attempt to share this revelation with you, but it will only make sense to you if you are willing to remove your parameters of earthly thinking. You must put on your eternity hat in order to get this. You must forget the constraints of logic and the limits of your own intelligence and exercise complete faith in God's supernatural word as the faith of a child who is willing to believe that God can do the impossible even if they can't explain how He does it. I'm not asking you to check your brain at the door, on the contrary, I'm asking you to consider the fact that God can and does work beyond the realm of human intelligence. *(Isaiah 55:9)* Ready? Onward....

The Deep Truth of Psalm 46

God is our refuge and strength, an ever-present help in trouble. (vs. 1)

Okay, if this is true then where was He when _____ happened? Fill in the blank. That situation or situations that have kept you bound in fear and pain your whole life, you know the one. The thing that in spite of all your efforts to believe that God is good and that His word is true, causes underlying doubt that keeps you from fully surrendering your heart to Him. So where was He? He was there, ever present and ready to help. But what if He couldn't help? What if He is restricted by His own spiritual laws and was unable to break them no matter how much He wanted to reach in and save you? This gets into the 'why do Christians suffer?' topic which is a subject for another book someday, but for now, you need to understand that God is bound by His own laws. He is not up in Heaven controlling people like puppets, and true love is not love at all unless its foundation is free will. That means that in order for God to be LOVE and for God to be TRUE, He cannot interpose His will against everything evil that happens on earth. Instead He sent JESUS so that those who love Him can step in and overcome the evil that comes against us and others! Unfortunately, most are not doing all they can. In reality, most are not doing anything at all and therefore the world suffers under the evil rule of Satan.

So let's talk about the here and now. Now you can know God's laws and your authority over evil. You can know His word and His promises to those who believe and if you know them you can use them right here, right now, even if you couldn't so long ago when you were abused, wounded, rejected or frightened.

Read Psalm 46 verse 1 again,

God is our refuge and strength, an ever-present help in trouble.

Jesus is an ever present help. He was present back then doing whatever He was legally allowed to do to help you survive, and He is present now waiting for you to invite Him to come and heal the wound that was caused so long ago. He is outside of time *(2 Timothy 1:9)* and therefore, it may be ten, twenty or fifty years later to you, but He can still be present on that very day, in this moment right here. *(2 Peter 3:8)*

Remember, this is a faith thing, your faith is the cause to the supernatural effect of your inner healing. Without the cause of faith, there can be no healing. I will explain the hows in just a minute but first let's move onto the next verse of Psalm 46...

> *"Therefore we will not fear, though the earth give way and the mountains fall into the heart of the sea, though its waters roar and foam and the mountains quake with their surging."*

(vs 2-3)

As you read through these scriptures, remember to read through the inner healing lens. God's word holds so many exciting mysteries, one of them is that every word was perfectly relevant for the time it was spoken, but it is also perfectly relevant for today. Another is that each scripture can and should be taken literally, but also holds deep spiritual truths and keys to connecting in spirit with it's Author, the God of Heaven.

When we look at this scripture from a literal standpoint we understand that it means exactly what it says. In that moment the writer, David, was expressing his faith in the Lord to the extent that he knew that even in the midst of an earthquake he would not fear. The word 'therefore' connects us to the why he would not fear from verse 1, because God is our refuge and strength, an ever present help in times of trouble. David knew that God would shelter & hide him, help him, and give him strength to survive even if the earth was thrown into utter chaos. He knew that God was always present to help. But since we know that

> *"all scripture is God breathed and useful for training us so that the servant of God may be complete, fully equipped for every good work...."*

(2 Timothy 3:16-17),

we must not only see what David was saying to God, but what God was prophetically saying to David and to us. It is thousands of years later to us, but to God, remember, He is out of time still speaking this in the present to every reader. Including YOU. It is being spoken to accomplish our training, completion and equipping. So what is He saying?

If your earth (foundation) has given way, your mountains (strength) seem to have drown amid a stormy sea that is raging and foaming with turmoil (trouble that threatens to overpower you), then you need not fear because Jesus is there, ready to help. Whether these things are happening now, will happen or have happened in the past, Jesus is there! Again, we will get to the how at the end of this chapter but for now I am setting the context for why this is my go to scripture for inner healing, stick with me. The next verse, the one at the beginning of this chapter, is my favorite!

"There is a river whose streams make glad the city of God, the holy place where the Most High dwells."

(vs. 4)

I seriously get tears in my eyes every time I read this scripture. We know by reading over eight hundred verses in scripture that Jerusalem is the city of God. This is how I have always read this scripture, until that early morning before my event when I sought the Lord for more understanding regarding inner healing. That morning it hit me, according to the New Testament *(1 Corinthians 3:16)*, I too am where the Most High dwells....there is a river who's streams make glad ME, the city of God!

What is This River?

The river is the Holy Spirit, we know this because when speaking to the multitudes before His death, Jesus called the Spirit 'rivers of living water.' *(John 7:37)* These rivers of living water are the supernatural power of the Holy Spirit in us who's flow makes us glad. I would be so bold as to say that if you are not glad and flowing in the fruit of the Spirit- love, joy (gladness), peace, patience, goodness, kindness, faithfulness, gentleness and self-control, then it is a direct result of something blocking the flow of the streams from the River.

Symptoms such as depression, anxiety, fear, rage, bitterness, lack of intimacy or conscience, addictions, physical illness and disease, and other kinds of brokenness are an indication that there there are areas in your soul or spirit and/or periods in your life where the River has not yet been given access.

Loved Children Shouldn't Beg

When we experience pain, sickness or emotional issues, most of us pray and ask God to 'take them away' or 'heal' us. We beg in prayer until we are blue in the face wondering why God won't answer. If this goes on long enough then we walk away either believing lies about God and His word, or lies about us- i.e. that we are unworthy of His help and healing. Both are twisted rhetoric of Satan and believing either will lead you into deeper bondage.

The truth is that by faith with the promises of scripture that we are His children *(John 1:12)*, we must seek to understand how the Father wants to partner with us for our emotional and spiritual healing. We must believe the truth of Psalm 46, Isaiah 53, 61 and so many other scriptures, enter into their supernatural reality by faith and meet with Jesus for the exchange. His joy for our sorrow, His beauty for our ashes, His identity for the false ones Satan has inflicted on us through trauma, abuse, rejection, loss and other pain & suffering.

We must do something to receive healing yes, but it is not about being good enough or working at it and this doesn't take years or even weeks. This is an instantaneous gift exchange. By your invitation Jesus comes to retrieve the pain & suffering you are carrying and He leaves you with freedom and your new identity in Him.

Each Other

> *"Therefore confess your sins to each other and pray for each other so that you may be healed. The prayer of a righteous man has great power to prevail."*
>
> *(James 5:16 BSB)*

I once heard someone on a radio program say, *"We have been hurt in relationship, so it makes sense that God would want to heal us in relationship."* That is pretty profound and I have seen it play out in my own life. Especially with my wonderful and godly husband, Randy.

A few months into our marriage, and after only having dated for three months to the day, my past rejection issues reared their ugly head in a huge way in an argument we were having. The funny thing is, I thought I had been healed of my past and didn't even know I still had rejection issues until I got married! It took a relationship to expose what had been silently festering under the surface when I was single for so many years. The Lord even gave me a profound dream to confirm that there were in fact emotional wounds in me that still needed healing. (I will be sure to share the dream in a video on the Emerald Ministries website at a future date.)

The evening of this particularly painful fight we were still in the throws of it heading into bed. In the midst of this my mind shifted from the emotional pain I felt Randy had [unintentionally] inflicted that afternoon to a phone call from someone else that I had gotten earlier. When my thoughts shifted the sobbing grew more intense. I retreated to the bathroom, embarrassed at the groaning that was coming out of me in raucous heaves that at some points didn't even sound human! I was more than crying, my spirit seemed to be unleashing years of deep, echoing sorrow. Up to that point Randy had been verbally fencing back and forth with me in matched vigor, then in the midst of my groaning I heard his voice, his words went from frustration and exasperation to genuine concern as he stopped mid-shout and called my name, asking if I was okay.

In that moment the Lord gave me clarity of why I was feeling the way I was. Something that was said on the phone earlier was the source of a rotten root that had been planted in me during my childhood. The situation with my husband triggered the pain and fear associated with that root, causing me to act crazy, and the crazier I acted the more sure I was that Randy thought he made a mistake marrying me. The old wound of rejection was manifesting in the ugliest way right in front of the one person I would never want to see it. But Randy was the very person that the Lord had chosen to minister to me His healing that night and in hindsight, I would not have it any other way.

Randy demanded I come out of the bathroom and led me in my sobs to the bed. He held me and softly prayed healing over my soul and spirit while the Lord did the supernatural surgery of pulling up the rotten root and rerooting me in His love until I could understand the depth of it according to scripture. *(Ephesians 3:17-18)*

This was the ugliest cry you can imagine! Snot was everywhere, the noises were inhuman and I distinctly remember wanting to run and hide as waves of fear and shame washed over me again and again. Randy's gentle, unconditional love kept me there so that Jesus could do His work, and this whole exchange laid a beautiful foundation for our marriage. This was as unappealing as I could ever imagine myself being and Randy loved me anyway, God knew that I needed that.

In this and other instances God knows that we need a human element to facilitate our healing with Jesus. Jesus could have healed my emotional wounds in my quiet time alone with Him that morning for sure, but then I still would've doubted Randy as a man going forward because of the pain that had been inflicted by other men. The complete healing came that day because Randy partnered with Jesus in loving me unconditionally and I partnered with Jesus in letting him.

Without Jesus, the healing would've been at a natural soul level for that time, place and relationship. Meaning that I may have trusted Randy's love after he proved it that day but the next time I perceived rejection from another person, that new person and every one after would have to prove their love as well because the rotten root would still be festering.

Without Randy the healing still would've been deep and lovely. I believe I could live free and healthy as an individual forever in that healing with Jesus. However, another type of mending between me and man would have been incomplete and needed to happen if I ever wanted to have a truly vulnerable and intimate relationship with my spouse or any other human again.

James 5:16, quoted at the start of this section, is not merely a suggestion, it is written as a command, *"Do this-so that."* So many people come against my inner healing & deliverance ministry stating that *"Jesus is the only healer and we need no one else, therefore I am spreading heresy and new age propaganda for personal gain."* I don't know what bible they are reading because this scripture and so many others are clear. Jesus want us to receive His healing through others that love and serve Him, and He wants us to go out and do the same for all we meet.

> *And as ye go, preach, saying, The kingdom of heaven is at hand. Heal the sick, cleanse the lepers, raise the dead, cast out devils: freely ye have received, freely give.'*
>
> *(Matthew 10:7-8 KJV)*

Time to Heal

If you are ready, I'd like to teach you some of the basic tools of Inner Healing now. Every exchange will look different because this is all about your love affair with Jesus and that doesn't look like my romance with Him or your pastor's, or spouse's or friend's, it is personal to YOU! Only He knows what you've been through and what you need from Him to heal and be whole again the way He intended. You can trust Him. Let's get started...

Your pre-session prayer should include asking the Lord to hide you in the shadow of His wings and send angels to do battle with you according to Psalm 91, and you should command that the enemy and all of his demons be silenced in Jesus's name according to your authority given in Luke 10:19 so that he cannot answer when you talk to the Lord. Then trust that your prayers have been answered. Proceed.

Step 1-Worship

"Enter his gates with thanksgiving, and his courts with praise! Give thanks to him; bless his name!"

(Psalm 100:4) (ESV)

The word says that God inhabits the praises of His people *(Psalm 22:3)*, we just learned that He inhabits us so what could this mean? Well, God is everywhere always so when the word says He inhabits the praises of His people it must mean something different happens than just God being present. It is His presence. In the Word, we see His presence manifest in all sorts of ways, including through angels, glory clouds, an audible voice, wind, fire, etc. And when the Lord's presence manifests, everything changes. When the Lord's presence manifest we know it in every fiber of our being.

There are people that go to church every week their whole lives, singing along with the worship leaders, yet they never experience God's manifest presence. I can't say exactly what is happening that prevents the Lord's presence from manifesting to us, but some of the factors could be unconfessed sin, pride, spiritual warfare, lack of knowledge to expect it or faith to receive it, wrong attitudes or half-hearted 'worship' and many other things.

He inhabits the praises, not the music. It is not enough to sing along to the nice words, we need to actually worship with the attitude that we are honoring the Lord and inviting Him to come and receive our offering of praise from us in Jesus's name.

Jesus told us that the Father is looking for those who will worship Him in spirit and truth *(John 4:23-24)*. Worshiping in spirit, with a lower case 's', means that our deepest part of us, our human spirit, the part where the Holy Spirit resides and connects us to heaven, must be called into action. Worship is not merely a soulish habit or exercise of the mouth and lungs but a spiritual offering to the Lord.

Call your spirit forth, literally, and make your soul-your mind, your will and your emotions-subject to what your spirit, in connection with the Holy Spirit, wants to do. Your spirit was created to worship, you just need to get your mind and will out of the way so it can lead. Once you do that, your soul will follow and thirst after more, for worshiping the Lord is your heart's deepest desire, most of us just don't realize it till it happens in spirit and truth.

Jesus said

"I am the way, the truth and the life."

(John 14:6)

So when He says the Father is seeking those who will worship in truth He is saying we are to worship 'in' Him. Meaning there is no other way, worship outside of Jesus and what He did for us means nothing. Worship without the humility that acknowledges Jesus and His death and resurrection is not worship-it is like handing the Creator of the universe filthy rags *(Isaiah 64:6)* and expecting Him to receive them as some kind of payment. Imagine going to the store for groceries and trying to pay for them with dirty rags insisting that they were the new currency! A grocery clerk would not be able to take rags as a form of payment and the Lord cannot take our good intentions as such either. The only currency with which our worship is heard in heaven is the blood of Jesus, the way, the truth and the life.

Worship is step one of inner healing because we are asking the Lord to come and be with us, we are welcoming Him to come and heal us from the inside out and He does that in close proximity to Him. Relationship means intimacy and intimacy requires closeness. Starting with worship draws us close to the Lord, and His word says that when we draw near to Him He will draw near to us. (James 4:8)

Step 2-Naming the Symptoms

"Surely he hath borne our griefs, and carried our sorrows..."

(Isaiah 53:4 KJV)

Now is the time to vocalize to the Lord what it is you want Him to carry away. Every pain, every grief, every sorrow, every symptom. It might sounds something like this, *"Jesus, your word says that you bore my griefs and sorrows. I have been carrying my own griefs and sorrows and I need You to come take them all. The anger, bitterness, depression, self hate/harm, suicidal thoughts, addictions, fear and anxiety, disease, etc. I'm giving You permission to come into every part of me, every thought, memory, and self protected place, I am welcoming You right now."*

Step 3-Uncovering the Rotten Roots

"For this reason I bow my knees before the Father, from whom every family in heaven and on earth derives its name, that He would grant you, according to the riches of His glory, to be strengthened with power through His Spirit in the inner man, so that Christ may dwell in your hearts through faith; and that you, being rooted and grounded in love, may be able to comprehend with all the saints what is the breadth and length and height and depth, and to know the love of Christ which surpasses knowledge, that you may be filled up to all the fullness of God. (Ephesians 3:14-19 NIV)

God wants us to be rooted and grounded in love and to know the love of Christ which surpasses knowledge, but life happens and the opposite is true for most. When painful things happen to us our spirit and soul become rooted in the pain and sin of the circumstances, then as we grow- we grow out of the soil of the pain, grief & sorrows and our theology is formed from such. Lies are believed about God and about ourselves and demonic strongholds are then created. Eventually we bear the rotten fruit of sins (bitterness, wrath, anger, clamor, slander, malice, etc.) and the rotten fruit of symptoms (fear, depression, cancer, anxiety, suicidal thoughts, eating disorders, auto immune diseases, addiction, etc.). All because we have roots grounded in rotten soil that was tilled by pain and is now defiled with demons. We need to pull up the rotten roots, establish new roots in the the love of Jesus and let him give our soul an overhaul. For this step you should start with the most pressing symptom, let's say depression for example. Ask the Holy Spirit to search the deepest places of your soul and spirit and to shine His light on the root of the depression (when it was first planted) to expose it. Then pay attention to what happens next.

Seeing

Are you seeing something? What does it look like? Who is there? Are you seeing an actual root? What is it planted in? What size or color is it? Processing what you see with Jesus will lead you down the path to the answer of what He wants to do. If you see a pink root planted in chocolate pudding you may be tempted to believe that you are making things up because that sounds crazy right? But don't dismiss anything! Ask Him what is going on! *"Lord, why is the root pink? Why is it planted in Chocolate pudding?"* Then LISTEN. He will tell you! He recently gave me a picture of crumpets that had nothing to do with the actual crumpets. When I asked Him why I was seeing crumpets He then spelled out the word in my mind and changed the little c to a capital K. As I said what I was seeing out loud the woman I was ministering to started laughing as she realized the Lord was calling her out on a horror movie she recently watched and needed to repent of! Do not dismiss what you are seeing, trust that He is answering!

Feeling

Are you feeling or sensing something? What emotion is prevalent in this moment? What do you want to do as you feel this? Stop? Run? Eat? The same applies here, process everything with Jesus. *"Lord why am I feeling like I want to run? Why am I feeling sadness? What are you trying to show me?"* If you feel fear for instance, then your depression could be rooted in fear! Ask Him! When feelings of fear, shame, sadness or rejection come up, you may be believing a lie, ask Him to reveal what lies you are believing. I witnessed one woman set free in an instant when the Lord revealed that she had been believing the lie that that the devil was bigger than God ever since watching the Exorcist movie when she was little! And I've met too many suffering from depression that was rooted in believing that they were unlovable or that their past abuse what their fault. These lies connected to wounds then cause sin symptoms like we saw in Ephesians 4, as well as demonic strongholds where the demons dwell instead of the Holy Spirit! YUCK! Whatever you are feeling-stay there with Jesus and process it with Him! Remember my story with my husband praying over me! I wanted to run as the shame and fear of rejection reared it's ugly head! Staying there with Jesus ministering to me through Randy is what allowed Him to complete the healing and root me in love. Stay put and let Him heal you no matter how difficult it is! It will only last a few moments and then the glorious freedom will come!

Are you hearing or 'thinking' something? Are words or thoughts running through your head? You know the drill, process this all with the Lord! Are you thinking, *"This is stupid. He's not going to show up and this is not going to work."* That is most likely the enemy testing you to see if you truly believed in your authority in Jesus when you commanded him to be silent in the beginning. Rebuke and silence him and start again.

Memories/Flashbacks

If you saw a memory, it is time to invite Jesus into that memory to bring justice and healing to your spirit and soul. Just ask Him, *"Jesus, please come and rescue me out of this?"* What He shows you next, just like in all the ways above, is HIM. (If you struggle with believing that He talks in this way, it would be a good idea to sign up for the Freedom Fighters Training Ground at Emerald Ministries where you can learn all about Imaginative Prayer.)

Healed Memory Example

I have a memory from when I was very little of my family being at an amusement park. We were going to ride the little train around the park and just before boarding I accidentally stepped in some vomit. I vividly remember everyone laughing and refusing to sit with me as a result of the smell. I sat alone in my own section feeling ashamed, embarrassed and rejected. My family couldn't have known the pain they were causing, they just thought it was funny, and being grown now I definitely see the humor! But at the time I had not yet developed the ability to laugh at myself and therefore took on this painful rejection as part of my identity. This incident created a rotten root in me that grew as I grew, helped to form my worldview and caused me to make some terrible decisions as a teen. I am not at all blaming my family for my later decisions, just showing how even something innocent like this amusement park incident can take root and and start to cause rotten fruit without us ever realizing that there is something that needs healing!

In this instance when I invite Jesus to come heal the pain of this memory, what He shows me is not only does He sit with me on the train, but He Himself cleans my shoes then hoists me up to sit on His right shoulder as He leads my family through the park. He put me in a place of honor and JOY with Him and now when I think of that memory, HE is all I see and joy is all I feel. Incredible.

The vomit incidence happened. Jesus did not turn back time and undo what happened. But what He did do is allow me to see into the spiritual dimension of the heavenlies where we are seated with Him *(Ephesians 2:6)*. He allowed me to experience in my spirit His beautiful love and justice by watching Him replace the rejection and shame with honor and joy. I am a forty seven year old woman sitting in my office writing this story. But I am also that five year old little girl sitting on Jesus's shoulder in complete, over the top bliss. It's all me. It's all now. What is no longer me is the girl no one would sit with on the train because Jesus sat with me. An ever present help in times of trouble. I didn't know how to see and invite Him to sit with me at the amusement park in 1975, but I do now and because of a little word called redemption, and His promise to restore what the locust has eaten *(Joel 2:25)*, this wound is healed and the memory has been redeemed. That is the power of the cross of Jesus Christ.

Conclusion

This chapter could just keep going and going, like I said at the beginning, learning all there is to know about inner healing is something that will most definitely be a life long journey for me. The Lord is continually revealing new tools and ways that He reaches in and binds up broken hearts. And I promise to continue to share them with you in the Freedom Fighters Training Grounds at Emerald Ministries as I get more and more revelation. In the meantime, the tools I shared in this chapter work as long as they are used in relationship with Jesus and with the motive of a pure heart that wants more of Him.

God's said in His word,

"My grace is sufficient for you."

(2 Corinthians 12:9)

Meaning, in His grace He has given us all we need to heal and be whole with Him and to take our authority over the enemy who is trying to steal, kill and destroy us. Praise the Lord! Now that our wounds are healed we move into the easiest part...kicking the bad guys out, finally! This is the 'overcoming' moment we've all been waiting for! So without further ado.....

WEAPON SIX:

DELIVERANCE

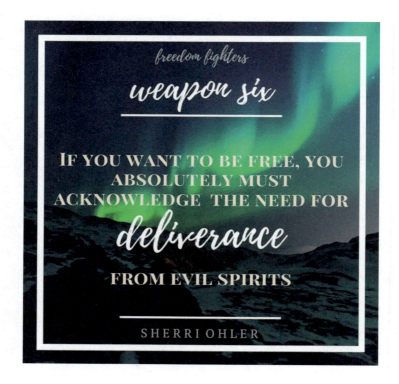

"For though we live in the flesh, we do not wage war according to the flesh. The weapons of our warfare are not the weapons of the world. Instead, they have divine power to demolish strongholds."

(2 Corinthians 10:3-4 BSB)

It is this author's belief that the reason Christians suffer with the same sins, diseases, addictions and brokenness as the rest of the world is because we for the most part have left behind Christ's teaching and mandate to cast out demons.

Look around and you will discover the that church as a whole wars according to the flesh. I can't tell you how many times I have heard of someone calling a church for help only to be referred to a counselor* for their issue! Unreal. Righteous anger rises even now as I think on this! What are we doing? Why have we settled for using mere weapons of the world and why are we disobeying Christ's mandate to cast out demons? *(Mark 16:16-18, John 14:11-13, Matthew 17:14-20, Luke 10:19, Matthew 17:19-20, John 14:12)* There are many answers to these questions but I am not here to critique the church as if I am doing everything right. Instead I am here to say enough is enough. To do my part to set the captives free and to teach others to do the same.

*In combination with deliverance, counseling can be a helpful tool in navigating life. But without deliverance, most often counseling is incomplete and a waste of time and money. Worst case scenarios even do more damage and enable a self-focused, victim mentality. If you want to understand more, see my YouTube video When to Seek Counseling vs When to Seek Inner Healing & Deliverance. Also watch for the Well Swimmers program coming soon to Emerald Ministries.

So, What Exactly is Deliverance?

Deliverance is the process of setting one free from the oppression of unclean spirits. Jesus spent much of his earthly ministry delivering people from evil spirits and gave His followers a mandate to do the same. Deliverance and Inner Healing are two sides of the same coin. Two of my favorite scriptures regarding our role in deliverance are below.

> *"Heal the sick, raise the dead, cleanse lepers, cast out demons. You received without paying; give without pay."*
>
> *(Matthew 10:8 ESV)*

And these signs will accompany those who believe: in my name they will cast out demons; *(Mark 16:17 ESV)*

Can a Christian Have Demons?

There is debate about whether Christians can be 'possessed' by demons and most have settled on the comfortable conclusion that they cannot.

I've heard it explained many times that 'Christians cannot be 'possessed' but they can be 'oppressed'. It is all semantics and unfortunately Satan has used this argument to keep Christians bound for centuries. He knew that if he could convince the church that they could not be possessed then they would look for other explanations for their problems and the demons would stay undetected. He succeeded triumphantly. And to be blunt, it disgusts me. The bible is very clear on the matter and the fact that so many have been convinced that they can't have demons tells me that the church is listening to man instead of God's word.

Look around at the problems of divorce, pornography, abuse, anger, addictions, depression, anxiety, fear, greed, homosexuality, etc. within the church and tell me there are not demons at play. People are more comfortable living a joyless life on prescription meds and blaming God for not healing them than they are being willing to admit they might have a demon problem. Denial is driven by fear and it is a vicious cycle.

Logic

Logically speaking we know that all our human problems do not dissipate just because we accept Jesus as Savior. Think about it. Addicts that say a salvation prayer still need to be set free from their addiction, cancer patients still need healing, people in broken marriages still must do the work to try to reconcile. Salvation doesn't instantly alleviate all our problems. The problems, and many times, the demons behind them are still present. Salvation doesn't make demons leave but what it does do is give us new weapons to fight with and new power to use them in Jesus. When Jesus told His disciples (and us) to go cast out demons, heal the sick, cleanse the lepers and raise the dead, salvation was a part of that. But if 'getting saved' is all that was needed, why did He tell us to do the rest? Why not just say, 'Go lead people through a salvation prayer.'?

> *"As you go, preach this message: '- The kingdom of heaven is near.' Heal the sick, raise the dead, cleanse the lepers, drive out demons."*
>
> *(Matthew 10:7-8 NIV)*

The logical answer is that salvation is one thing and deliverance is another. So, here's my resounding answer, YES, Christians can have demons! If you want to be free you absolutely must acknowledge the need for the deliverance from evil spirits. Now let's look at that 'possessed' word.

Possessed? Oppressed? Something Else?

The best theology I have ever heard about demons was on a bus in Brazil in a conversation with Global Awakening Leader, Blaine Cook. He said, 'I don't care if the demons are in me, on me or around me, I just want them gone." Amen brother. Who cares where they are, if they are affecting me they need to GO!

But since people are so hung up on this issue, let's discuss it further. The word in the King James bible where we get the language and understanding of 'demon possession' from is *daimonizomai*. It is Greek and it means, 'to have a devil or to be vexed by a devil'. Yes, Christians are vexed by devils. Period.

To get technical, if I have a house that I live in one could say that I possess the house. As in, possession is 9/10ths of the law. If I am in it then I possess it. In this sense, demons could say they possess humans because they live in them.

To use the same house analogy, salvation is like giving the demons an eviction notice. Like any experienced squatter they will stay and fight until they are physically forced out. It is not enough to just put them on notice, we must force them leave!

For scriptural evidence that Christians can have demons, read the story of Jesus's interaction with the woman whose daughter was demon possessed in Matthew 15. She comes begging for help because her daughter is 'terribly possessed' by a demon but Jesus tells her that it is not right to give the children's bread to the dogs. He was not being derogatory as it would be today to speak that way. He was saying that DELIVERANCE is intended for God's children and that it would be wrong to deliver someone who was not God's child. A dog is dependent upon its master for food, water and care and Jesus knew that without Him as her (and her daughter's) master, she would be susceptible to worse possession. (See Matthew 12:45) Her response was all He needed to set her daughter free in that very hour.

> *"Yes, Lord, she said, "- even the dogs eat the crumbs that fall from their master's table."*
>
> *(vs. 27, BSB)*

She recognized Him as Master, became one of His children in that very moment and therefore her family was ready to receive deliverance. As you can see, scripturally, deliverance is for God's children. It is quite the opposite of scripture to say that Christians cannot be possessed by demons. That is a lie of the devil himself.

Two Ways to Be Delivered

At first glance what I am about to say might sound like I am contradicting the last section, but stick with me and it will make sense. I believe that we can be delivered through Sanctification, or the act of becoming more Christ-like. Not because of natural behavior but because of heavenly position and proximity.

> *"Now the Lord is the Spirit, and where the Spirit of the Lord is, there is freedom. And we, who with unveiled faces all reflect the glory of the Lord, are being transformed into His image with intensifying glory, which comes from the Lord, who is the Spirit."*
>
> *(2 Corinthians 3:17-18)*

We are being transformed by the Holy Spirit into greater levels of His glory! Other translations say, 'from glory to glory'! I personally have been delivered of demons just by getting to the next level of glory in Him. Had I known they were there I would've sought out someone who knew how to minister the Lord's deliverance. Instead, I suffered with them until the Lord drew me to places where He could make them leave. So, the two ways of deliverance are either we make the demons leave in His name, or we wait until we are in a position with Him where He is legally allowed to drive them out because of our sanctification. Both are forceful, purposeful evictions. But knowing what I know now, I would recommend forcing them to leave in His name as He told us to do. There is no reason to wait.

Knowing the Demon's Name

Some people approach deliverance assuming they need to find out the demon or demons names based on the story of the Gadarenes man in the tombs from Luke chapter 8.

> *"26 Then they sailed to the country of the Gadarenes, which is opposite Galilee. 27 And when He stepped out on the land, there met Him a certain man from the city who had demons for a long time. And he wore no clothes, nor did he live in a house but in the tombs. 28 When he saw Jesus, he cried out, fell down before Him, and with a loud voice*

> *said, "What have I to do with You, Jesus, Son of the Most High God? I beg You, do not torment me!" 29 For He had commanded the unclean spirit to come out of the man. For it had often seized him, and he was kept under guard, bound with chains and shackles; and he broke the bonds and was driven by the demon into the wilderness. 30 Jesus asked him, saying, "What is your name?" And he said, "Legion," because many demons had entered him."*
>
> *(Luke 8:26-30 NKJV)*

Many believe that Jesus was talking to the man when he asked his name, but instead of the man, the demons answered. Many other point to this to say that we need to know the demon's name before we can command them to leave. I am somewhere in the middle. I do not know if Jesus was talking to the man or the demons, and there are times the Holy Spirit tells me the names of the demons I am dealing with, but I never have purposely asked a demon a question. I'm not saying that couldn't happen, but to this point that has not been necessary. My interaction during deliverance is solely with the Lord and the person receiving ministry until it is time to command the demons to be quiet, release the person from 'in the moment' affliction, or cast them out completely.

The Holy Spirit has only given me the name of the demon I was dealing with a couple of times. In the first situation, this knowledge gave us breakthrough and freedom from an issue the woman was tiptoeing around. It was like the Holy Spirit knew we'd never get there so He gave me the name to call it out so it couldn't hide any longer. The second situation led me to understand the demon behind the particular eating disorder a woman was dealing with so we knew what she needed to renounce and what the demons motives were.

The common denominator in both scenarios is that the name gave me a clue about what I was dealing with, just as it did Jesus. Jesus knew by the name, Legion, that there were many. I knew by the names the Holy Spirit revealed to me what the sins and mindsets were that had allowed the demons to stay to this point. However, more often than not it is sufficient to call the demon by its manifestation symptoms. For example, spirit of heaviness/depression, fear/anxiety, witchcraft/addiction/control, lust, cancer, etc.

I considered giving the names of the two above examples here, but I think there is more discussion to be had about them than I can cover here so I will tell the stories in the Freedom Fighters Training Grounds -Deliverance Arena. To write the names here would be to puff them up and I will not give the enemy the satisfaction.

What Deliverance Ministry is Truly About

The truth about any deliverance session is that it is all about your relationship with the Jesus. He will tell you what is going on and how to deal with it moment by moment. The rule is that demons are attached to sin and woundedness so we first deal with those things, remove their legal right to stay and then, in Jesus's name they must leave very quietly. To cast them out without first dealing with the roots will lead to an unnecessary battle of wills between you, the person you are ministering to, and the demons themselves. When deliverance ministers take this approach, I believe there is pride involved. They like seeing the demons writhe and fight and ultimately succumb to the authority of the minister. Many times, in this type of deliverance the demons then cause the minister-ee to vomit, writhe, scream, curse, etc. It is so unnecessary. There are biblical examples of people quickly convulsing when Jesus cast out demons, so that is normal, as is a little coughing, but anything more than that is your clue to take back control and backtrack a bit. In a situation like this, bind the demon from manifesting in the name of Jesus, then back up and see what legal right he or they still have by following the leading of the Holy Spirit.

Long time deliverance minister, pastor and author, Derick Prince recommends telling the person to blow out when it is finally time to cast out the demon. I have found this helpful and use it in my ministry. It is an act of the persons will and a step of faith that just helps the whole process. During this blowing a little coughing is normal as the demons come up and out.

The Devil's Method of Deliverance

I recently watched a YouTube video where a so called 'minister' commanded 'angels' to beat up a demon that was still within a person. He talked about how his 'angels' listen to his every command and then said, *"Watch this..."* as he proceeded to cause the 'angels' to toss the man around on the floor again and again all while filming his so-called display of spiritual power in Jesus's name. It was awful and not of God. How do I know? Because it was completely void of LOVE. The minister had no compassion or love for the victim. He, like the demon, was using him for his own pleasure and personal gain. I guarantee that was not a heavenly angel that he was commanding, but his own personal evil spirit.

When ministering in deliverance our number one priority is taking care of the person we are ministering to. We should seek to love them with the love of Christ, to ease their fears and to help them the best we can to walk away full of Holy Spirit power and His fruit of love, joy, peace, patience, kindness, goodness, faithfulness, gentleness, and self-control. *(Galatians 5:22-23)*

According to Jesus, our reason to rejoice is not that we have power over the enemy, although that is something to celebrate for sure, deliverance is about our names being written in heaven! It is because our names are in heaven that the demons must listen to us, not the other way around.

> *"Nevertheless, do not rejoice that the spirits submit to you, but rejoice that your names are written in heaven."*
>
> *(Luke 10:20 NIV)*

Is Deliverance Ministry Dangerous?

The simple answer is yes, if you do not know your identity in Christ, how to hear His voice and have faith in your God given authority over the evil one. And no, absolutely not if you know who you are in Christ, who He is in you, and your total authority over the enemy and his minions.

I recently ministered to a woman whose demon started shaking in fear of little old me when she walked into the room for her session. He knew what was about to happen and turned into a quivering lump. To put it humorously, I had him at hello! We made him leave and later I received a message from her that she was shocked at what happened and frustrated with herself that this weak spirit held so much power over her for decades.

The devil's game is all smoke and mirrors. Truly. If he can convince us he is scary and more powerful than we are or than God is, then he is more powerful because we just gave up our faith and surrendered our authority. In actuality he will always be nothing compared to our awesome

God! But that is irrelevant. The only thing that matters is what we believe about him and about God. It is the knowledge of the truth (about both) that sets us free! *(John 8:32)*

We see this very thing play out in scripture in the story of the sons of Sceva...

> *"And God was doing extraordinary miracles by the hands of Paul, 12 so that even handkerchiefs or aprons that had touched his skin were carried away to the sick, and their diseases left them and the evil spirits came out of them. 13 Then some of the itinerant Jewish exorcists undertook to invoke the name of the Lord Jesus over those who had evil spirits, saying, "I adjure you by the Jesus whom Paul proclaims." 14 Seven sons of a Jewish high priest named Sceva were doing this. 15 But the evil spirit answered them, "Jesus I know, and Paul I recognize, but who are you?" 16 And the man in whom was the evil spirit leaped on them, mastered all of them and overpowered them, so that they fled out of that house naked and wounded."*
>
> *(Acts 19:11-12 ESV)*

Naked & wounded! Yikes! Paul knew who he was, he had an amazing relationship with the Lord and was willing to give everything to serve Him. On the contrary, the sons of Sceva were imitating Paul and didn't even know Jesus. Demons may be weak in the presence of a Spirit filled lover of Jesus, but they aren't so stupid as to not know when someone is just using His name without really knowing Him. The bottom line is that all ministry we do should be born out of our love for and relationship with Jesus. When that is the case, there is nothing at all to fear.

Let's Do This

If you believe that you have demons and have gone through all the other steps in the book in relationship with Jesus Christ, you are now ready to make the demons leave and it should be quite simple.

Step 1- Pray and ask the Lord to send His angels to protect you, your family and property and to do battle on your behalf if necessary. *(Hebrews 1:14)*

Step 2- Enter God's presence through worship. (Psalm 100:4)

Step 3- Command the demon to come out by its symptom name, in Jesus' name, then blow out. For example, *"I command you unholy spirit of heaviness and depression to loose me in the name of Jesus, come out of me now! I belong to Jesus!"*

Step 4- Tell it where to go. Literally. By default, I say, *"Go to where Jesus tells you to go without touching or harming anyone."* Repeat Steps 3 & 4 for every symptom.

Step 5- Ask the Holy Spirit to shine His light to reveal any more that may be hiding, repeat Steps 3 & 4 again until He says you are clean. Then invite Him to come in and fill you with the opposite! If you suffered from lust, ask for Holy Spirit purity, depression-joy, fear-love!

Enjoy this time with Him, don't rush, this is the fun part! Ask the Lord to show you a picture of what you look like now. People have seen themselves bathing in glorious waterfalls, flying with the Holy Spirit or sitting on Abba Father's lap and so much more! Who knows what He will show you! Embrace your new, closer relationship with the Lord and stay in the moment as long as you like. Praise, praise, praise His holy name!

Step 6- Ask the Father to clean out all the surrounding space in the building or area you are in and to make sure that no straggling spirits are hanging around trying to reattach to you, your property, animals or anyone else. In faith, know He answered.

Now it's time to enjoy your new-found freedom and to learn to go on the offensive. You are about to turn the tables on the enemy with a crash course in spiritual warfare. Onward!

A New Calling: Spiritual Warfare

"And they have conquered him by the blood of the Lamb and by the word of their testimony, for they loved not their lives even unto death."

(Rev. 12:11)

There are so many scriptures I could have started this chapter with. And obviously like the other chapters, I could write entire books on Spiritual Warfare because there is so much to cover on the topic in God's word. But this is the scripture that the Lord has been speaking to me since I wrote the first word of the Freedom Fighters Introduction and I believe it sums up our role in warfare perfectly.

This chapter is going to cover pretty much just the bottom line when it comes to Spiritual Warfare. The way that we overcome Satan is by the blood of Jesus Christ, by vocalizing all He has done and finally, by not clinging too tightly to our earthly lives. In other words, we overcome by being 'eternity minded' in everything. All other things regarding spiritual warfare flow out of this mindset.

The Blood of the Lamb

This entire book is peppered with references to the blood of Christ, but it is worth repeating and expounding on a bit because without it, we have nothing. It is Christ's shed blood that gives us the hope of heaven, the power to heal, the remission of sins, a new peace & joy filled life on earth, and so much more.

Without the blood of the Lamb there is no Christianity. Without the blood we are nothing but fodder for Satan's evil plans and purposes for humanity! Truly. The word says that,

"Satan prowls around like a roaring lion, seeking someone to devour."

(1 Peter 5:8) (ESV)

The reason that we are not fully consumed by him unto eternal death is only because Christ shed His blood in our place, sparing our lives. But that doesn't mean that the devil can't kill us here in the physical as you will see as we go on. This is where warfare comes in. The blood is not only for our entrance into heaven, it is intended to defeat the enemy on earth as well! The blood draws a line that the enemy can't cross, but like anything else, it takes faith, good theology and understanding of God's promises to activate it. It is by your profession of faith in Christ's blood to save you- that you are saved, and it will be by your profession of faith in the blood to overcome sickness, death, destruction, poverty, depression, fear, etc., etc., etc. that you will overcome.

Communion

"For as often as you eat this bread and drink the cup, you proclaim the Lord's death until he comes."

(1 Corinthians 11:26 ESV)

There is deep revelation about communion that I am still seeking and probably will be until I am with Him in Heaven! But I will pass on what I have gleaned from the Lord thus far. I have been reading 1 Corinthians chapter 11 regarding communion over and over and honestly, it does not seem to be referring to 'communion' in the way that we think of it. There is a spiritual principal here that we will over look if we just assume it means wafers and little cups of grape juice. When we dig deeper we see how this chapter holds a spiritual warfare key that connects us to the Revelation 12 verse from the beginning of this chapter.

"When you come together, it is not the Lord's supper that you eat."

(vs. 20 ESV)

The original word here for supper is, deipnon. It means dinner, the chief meal, feast. Through theological study by those way smarter than me, this word has been found to be used in scripture as symbolizing the Messiah's feast and salvation in the kingdom. Therefore we need to read this chapter realizing that Paul was talking to believers that were coming together for a large meal as the body of Christ to remember His salvation. The eating of wafers and grape juice or wine is symbolic of an actual shared meal. Even when Jesus first broke the bread and taught that it was His body broken and His blood shed, they were gathered for the Passover meal, not just wafers and wine. It is no different here, they were coming together as professed believers for real supper. Paul goes on to reprimand these believers because some were going hungry and others were getting drunk. If there were just little pieces of bread and enough wine for little sips no one would be able to get full or drunk. This can only mean that it wasn't how they were taking 'communion' as we think of it that was the problem, but it was their hearts regarding salvation and each other (the body of Christ).

Earlier in verses 18-19 Paul states that they came together for worse instead of better. That there were factions or divisions among them. This is why he said, *"It is not the Lord's supper that you eat." (vs 20)* Because they were not coming together in a worthy matter of those that have been saved by the broken body and shed blood of Christ. They were selfish, gluttonous, and divisive. This was NOT the Lord's salvation.

Jumping ahead to verses 27-30 we read, *"Whoever, therefore, eats the bread or drinks the cup of the Lord in an unworthy manner will be guilty concerning the body and blood of the Lord. Let a person examine himself, then, and so eat of the bread and drink of the cup. For anyone who eats and drinks without discerning the body eats and drinks judgment on himself. That is why many of you are weak and ill, and some have died."*

Weak, ill and DEAD! Hello! I'm thinking this is a verse we may want to understand. The word here for judgment can also be mean condemnation or punishment. Since Jesus said

"For God did not send his Son into the world to condemn the world, but to save the world through him."

(John 3:17 NIV)

We can understand that the judgment that we can bring upon ourselves is not God's judgment. Rather we can choose to step out from under God's umbrella of grace and instead stand under the downpour of condemnation of the enemy. So how exactly does one do that? Stay with me...

I have only ever heard these passages of 1 Corinthians 11 taught regarding examining your heart and repenting before getting in line for communion. I think that is a very shortsighted understanding of what Paul is really getting at. That theology is akin to sinning all week then heading to confession with a priest to get cleaned up a couple times a month! No, cleaning up before downing a wafer called 'communion' is not what Paul meant at all. He was speaking of taking part in what Christ accomplished on the cross. Feasting on the bread and cup of the new covenant of the suffering of Jesus's body and the shedding of Jesus's blood. He was talking about partaking of SALVATION and all that comes with that.

Do we partake of salvation is an unworthy manner? Do we think that we can profess Christ and yet continue in selfishness? Disregarding the rest of the body of Christ? Can we cause division among Christ's body and get away with it? Clearly this scripture says that we cannot. If we want to come to the Lord's feast (the benefits of salvation on earth) through His body and blood we must do so in a worthy manner.

"For as often as you eat this bread and drink the cup, (partake of the benefits of salvation) you proclaim the Lord's death (the power of the shed blood) until he comes."

(1 Corinthians 11:26)

Since we know that salvation is a free gift and not a result of our own works according to Ephesians 2:8-9, we know that this verse is not talking about being good enough to receive salvation. But rather, once saved it is a matter of honoring what Christ did for us on the cross by living in a manner worthy of His sacrifice. By employing the blood as a means to live holy and overcome the enemy we thereby proclaim Jesus's death until He comes. The blood speaks for itself when we accomplish by faith what Christ intended us to accomplish on the earth!

We honor Him in our salvation by not taking His grace for granted, by loving His body and overcoming the enemy. When we embrace and move in the benefits of salvation-holiness, healing, deliverance, miracles, the fruit of the Spirit, raising the dead, cleansing the lepers, etc. we loudly proclaim His death through the demonstration of the power of the blood! This -is overcoming by the blood of the Lamb according to Revelation 12. Praise Jesus!!!!!

The Word of Their Testimony

"...for the testimony of Jesus is the spirit of prophecy."

(Revelation 19:10 KJV)

Did you know that your personal testimony of what Jesus has done carries the very spirit (breath or life) of prophecy (God's divine purposes)? What does that mean? It means that when you tell the story of what Jesus has done for you, you are breathing God's divine purpose into your life, the lives of those listening and the world in general. To put it another way, if every person on the planet stopped talking about what Jesus has done and is doing, then God's purposes on the earth would cease moving forward. His purposes would still stand but since He has chosen US to move them forward by preaching the Gospel, they would cease until someone was faithful to the call to speak of what He has done! We have a mandate to preach the good news *(Matthew 28:19-20)*! This is why the enemy tries to shut up God's people through shame, intimidation, distractions, etc.! When you share the good news of what Jesus has done, you are speaking life, faith, blessing, hope, power, love and God's purposes into motion! And in turn you OVERCOME THE ENEMY.

When God's purposes move forward the enemy's plans are stopped. We see no clearer picture of this than that of the cross. Satan's plan was to kill Jesus so that He could not save the world. But when Jesus's death and resurrection happened the enemy's plans to prohibit salvation were crushed as the Father's call and purpose for Jesus's life and death moved forward . In your own life God has a call and purpose that Satan wants to kill, steal and destroy. *(John 10:10)* When you are moving forward in the call and purposes of God for your life, the enemy's plans for you cannot prevail. Whether Satan's plans include cancer, divorce, depression, poverty, fear, addiction etc., his plans cannot succeed when you are in the center of God's will and purpose for your life. When Satan attacks through these things it is a natural reaction to shift our focus to the problem and to stop sharing our testimony as we deal with the battle. But the battle is overcome by keeping our eyes fixed on Jesus and sharing all He has done and is doing. We overcome by the word of our testimony!

In many places of the world and throughout history people are being persecuted unto death for sharing their testimony! This is why this verse ends with, *"for they loved not their lives even unto death."* Because if we love our earthly life so much that we go quiet in the face of persecution from the enemy through spiritual or natural attacks-we have not overcome the enemy-rather, he has overcome us. Jesus said *"Anyone who loves their life will lose it, while anyone who hates their life in this world will keep it for eternal life." (John 12:25 NIV)* When we are eternity minded we are all about spreading the good news of Jesus Christ to the ends of the earth (even if the end of the earth for us is our very own neighborhood)! It seems counterproductive as many times what puts us on the front lines of enemy battle is the Gospel! BUT, these are not natural laws, they are supernatural and as such the outcome is the opposite of what it seems. If you lose your life you will keep it for eternity.

Like I said at the beginning of this chapter, this is the bottom line of warfare. The little ins and outs of how to battle* are important, yes, but if I spelled them all out for you and you did everything 'right' but your life wasn't about the blood of the Lamb and sharing His good news, no training in spiritual warfare would ever work. On the contrary a life filled with passion for sharing all that Jesus has done is a life with the perfect foundation for victory in every battle. This is why I called this chapter A New Calling. Before you are free your life is about struggles, problems, troubles & issues. But when you get free your life is about Jesus, telling His good news and sharing the same freedom with others who are bound as you once were.

Your new calling is FREEDOM FIGTHER and from now on spiritual warfare shall be filled with joy as you proclaim His death and set the captives free! No longer are you weary of life, but His joy becomes your strength, and His Gospel your purpose & weapon to overcome! *(Nehemiah 8:10, Philippians 1:21)*

May you be blessed in every step of your journey, free in every area of your life, and joyous in every battle. In Jesus's holy name. Amen.

*If you'd like to know more about the how to's of Spiritual Warfare, Hearing the Voice of the Lord, Inner Healing & Deliverance Ministry, Spiritual Gifts, Biblical Healing with Anointing Oils, and Natural Medicine, Recipes and more, please visit emeraldglorywellness.com, and follow on Facebook and Tiktok http://tiktok.com/emeraldglorywellness.

Made in the USA
Columbia, SC
02 March 2025

54594054R00046